JALISCO

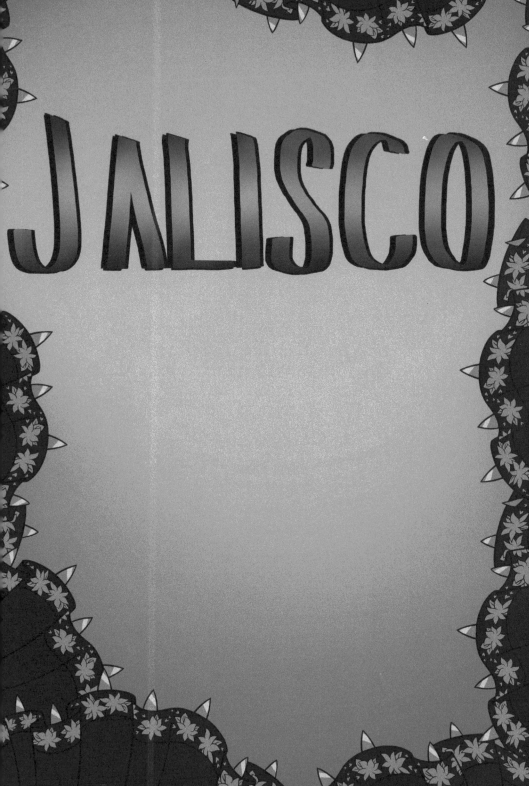

JALISCO, December 2019

Published by Phoenix Studios, LLC

Second Edition, 2019

ISBN: 978-1-7339093-2-7

JALISCO

WRITTEN BY	KAYDEN PHOENIX
ART BY	AMANDA JULINA GONZALEZ
INKING BY	HANNAH DIAZ
COLORING BY	MIRELLE ORTEGA ADDY RIVERA SONDA GLORIA FELIX
LETTERING BY	SANDRA ROMERO

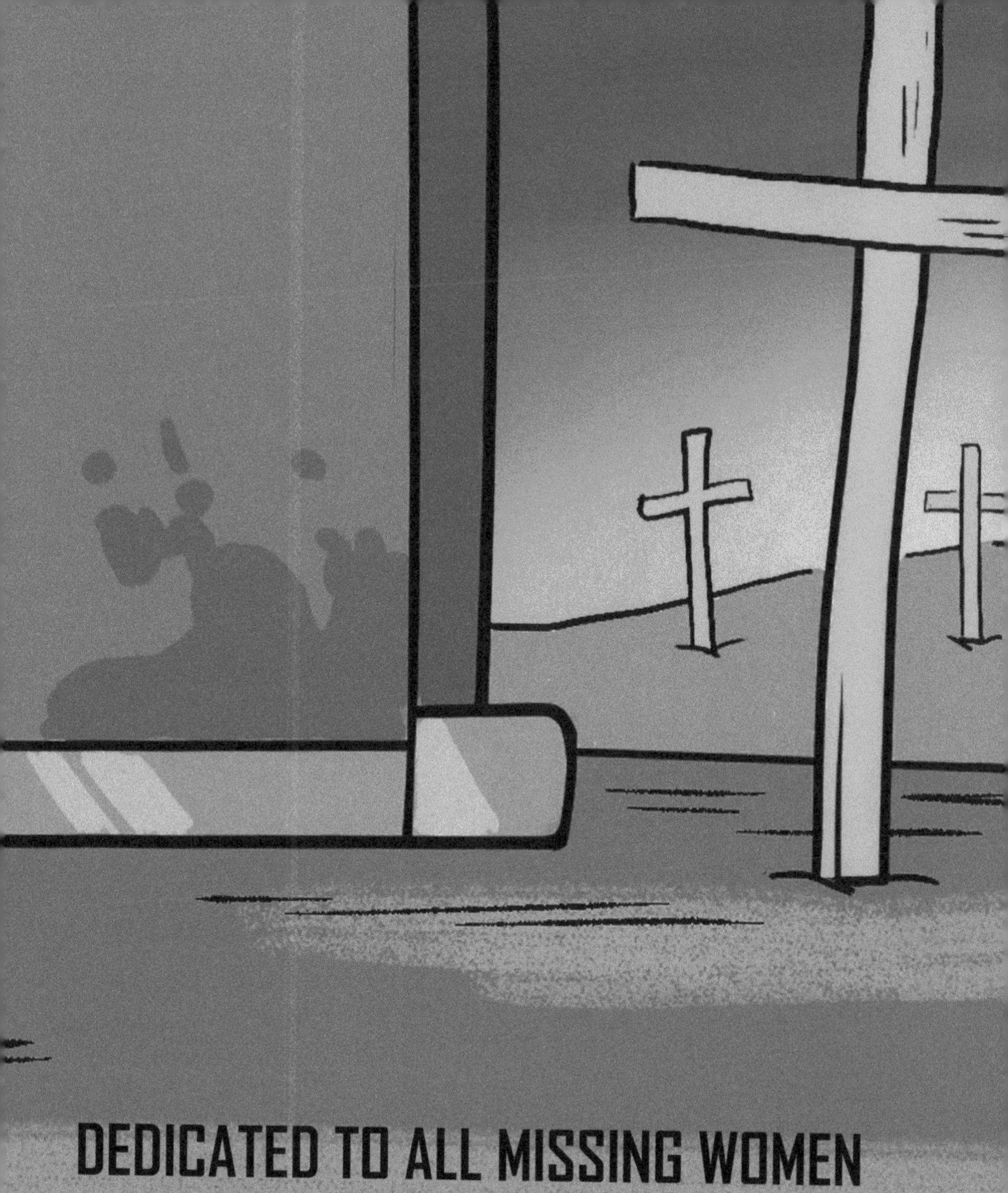

DEDICATED TO ALL MISSING WOMEN

CHAPTER 1

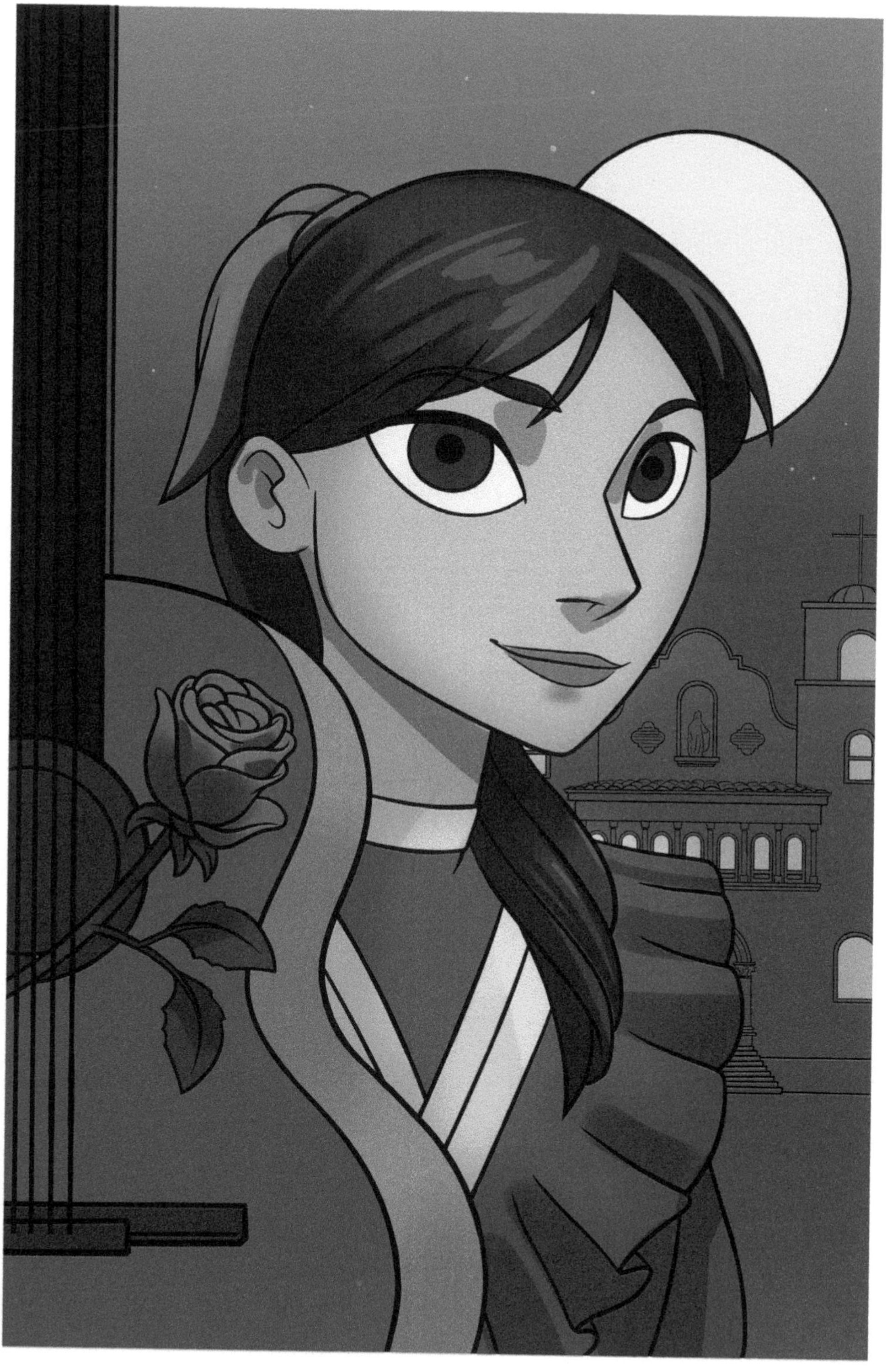

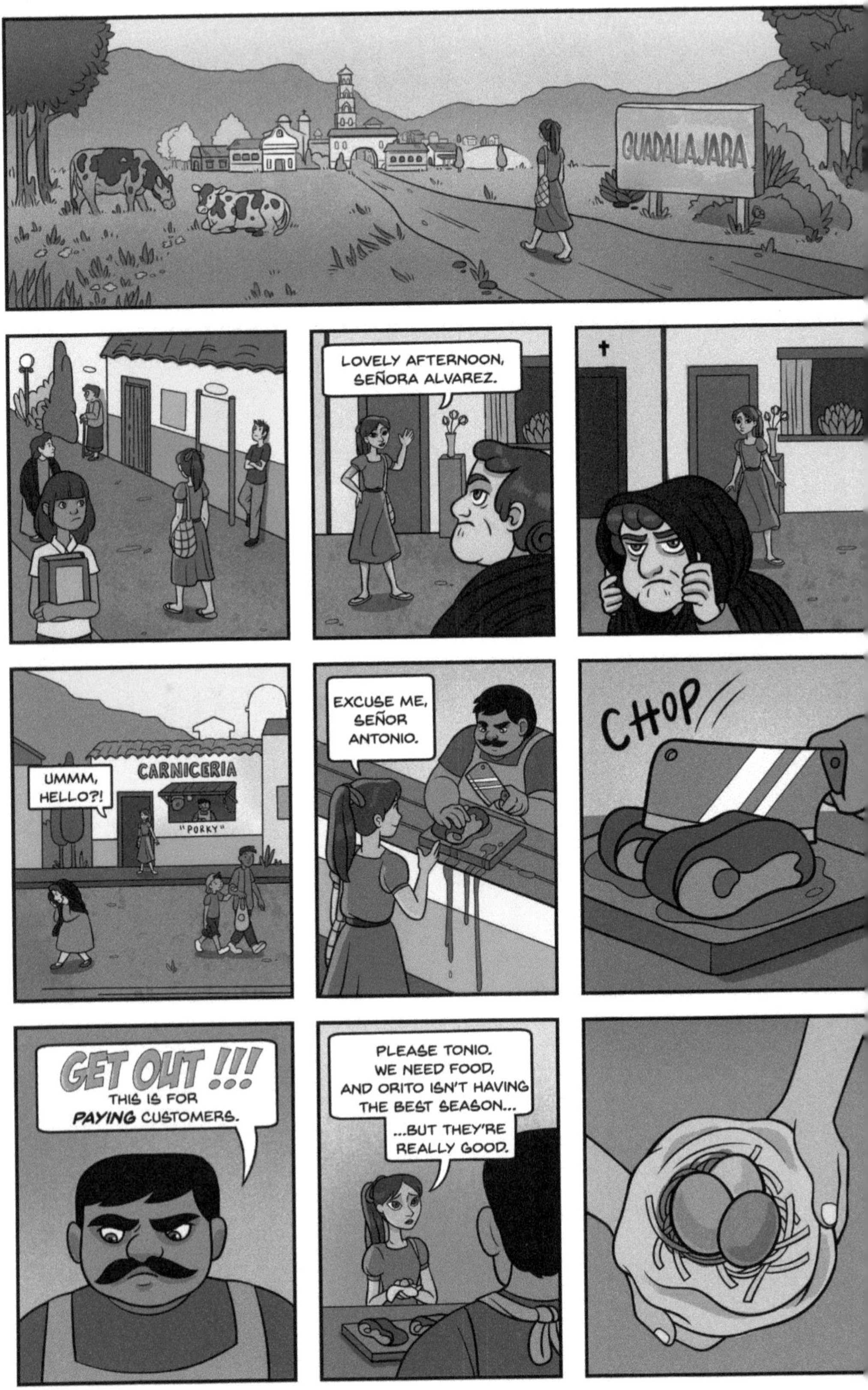
GUADALAJARA
LOVELY AFTERNOON, SEÑORA ALVAREZ.
CARNICERIA
"PORKY"
UMMM, HELLO?!
EXCUSE ME, SEÑOR ANTONIO.
CHOP
GET OUT !!! THIS IS FOR PAYING CUSTOMERS.
PLEASE TONIO. WE NEED FOOD, AND ORITO ISN'T HAVING THE BEST SEASON...
...BUT THEY'RE REALLY GOOD.

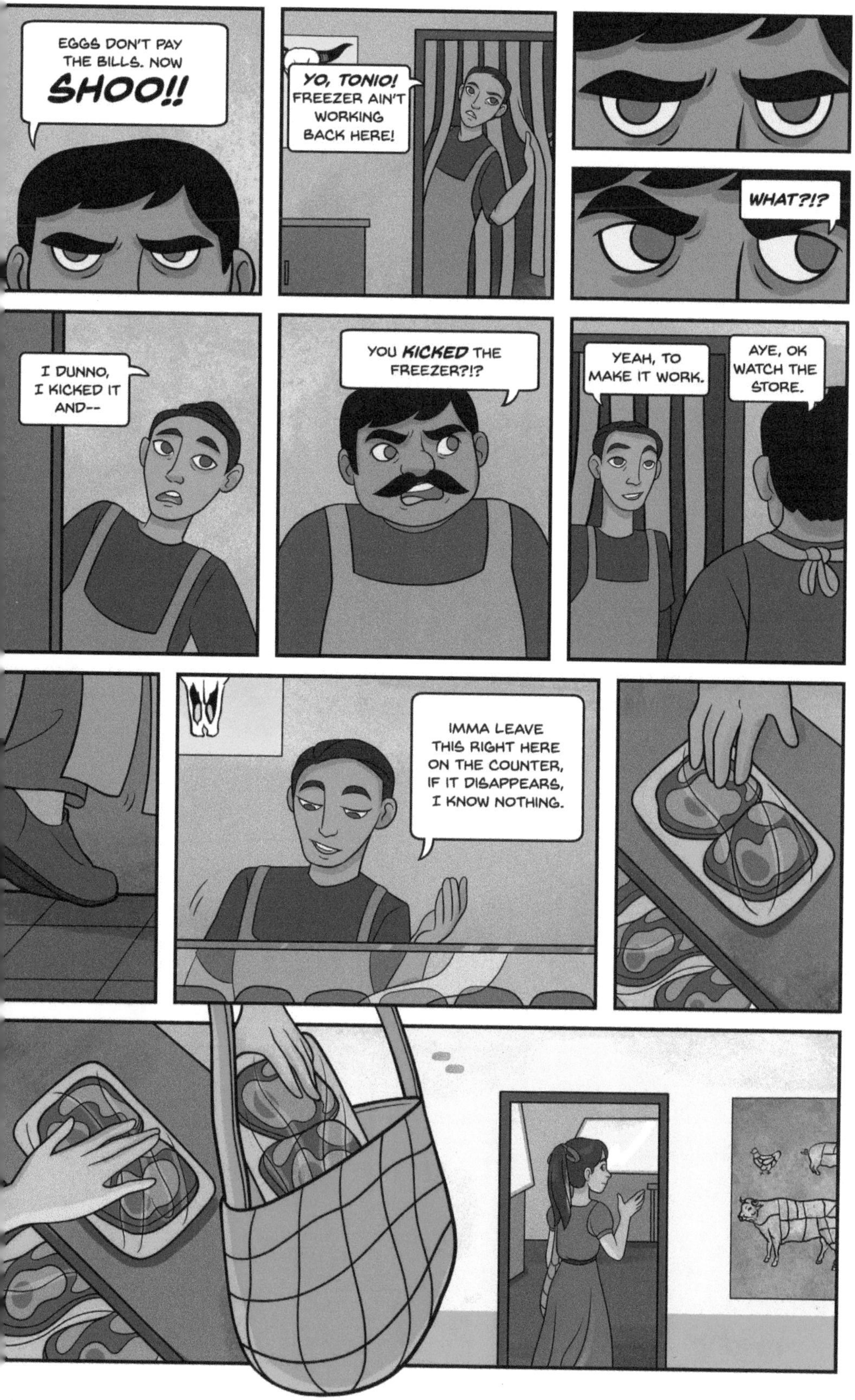
EGGS DON'T PAY THE BILLS. NOW SHOO!!
YO, TONIO! FREEZER AIN'T WORKING BACK HERE!
WHAT?!?
I DUNNO, I KICKED IT AND--
YOU KICKED THE FREEZER?!?
YEAH, TO MAKE IT WORK.
AYE, OK WATCH THE STORE.
IMMA LEAVE THIS RIGHT HERE ON THE COUNTER, IF IT DISAPPEARS, I KNOW NOTHING.

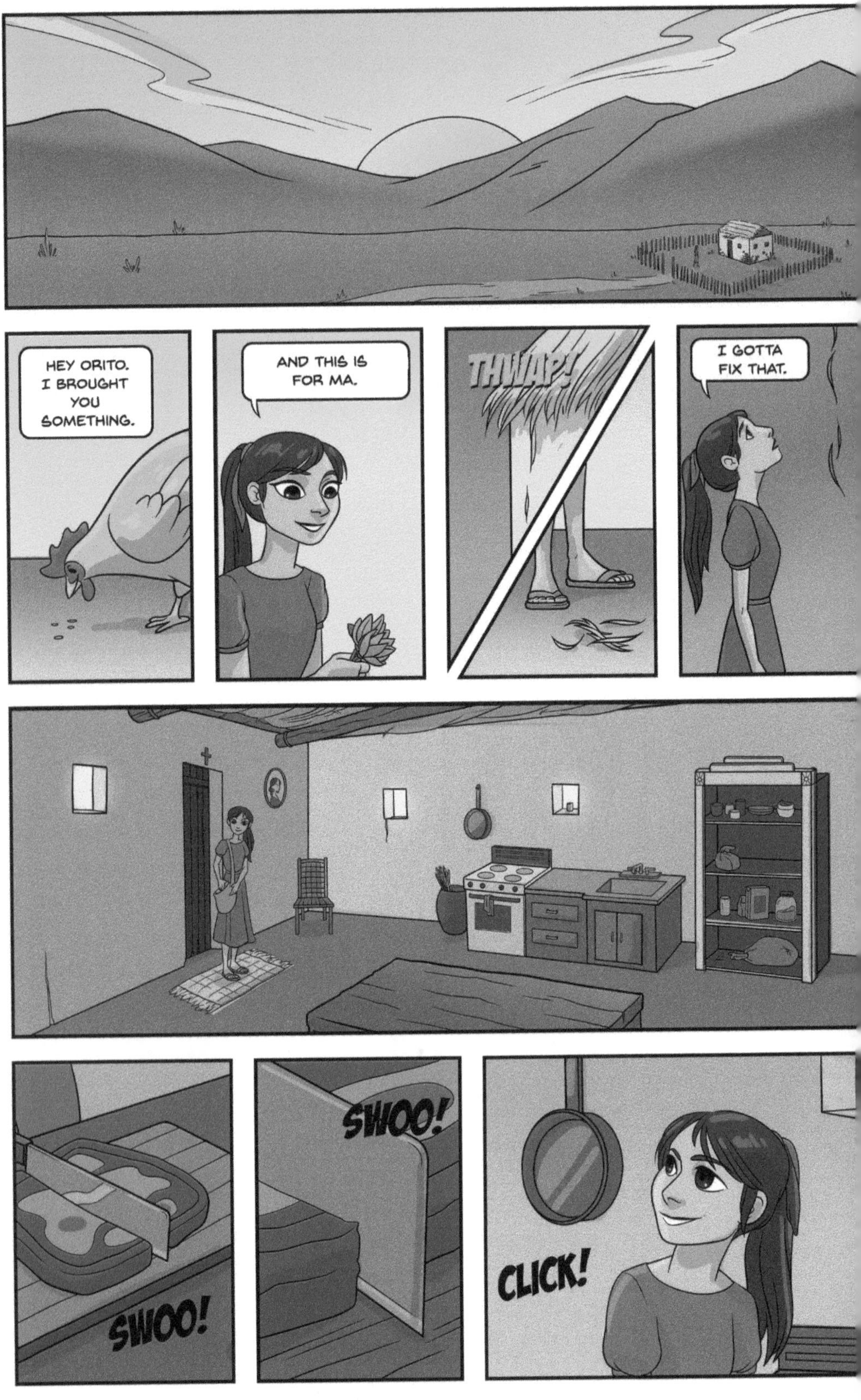
HEY ORITO. I BROUGHT YOU SOMETHING.
AND THIS IS FOR MA.
THWAP!
I GOTTA FIX THAT.
SWOO!
SWOO!
CLICK!

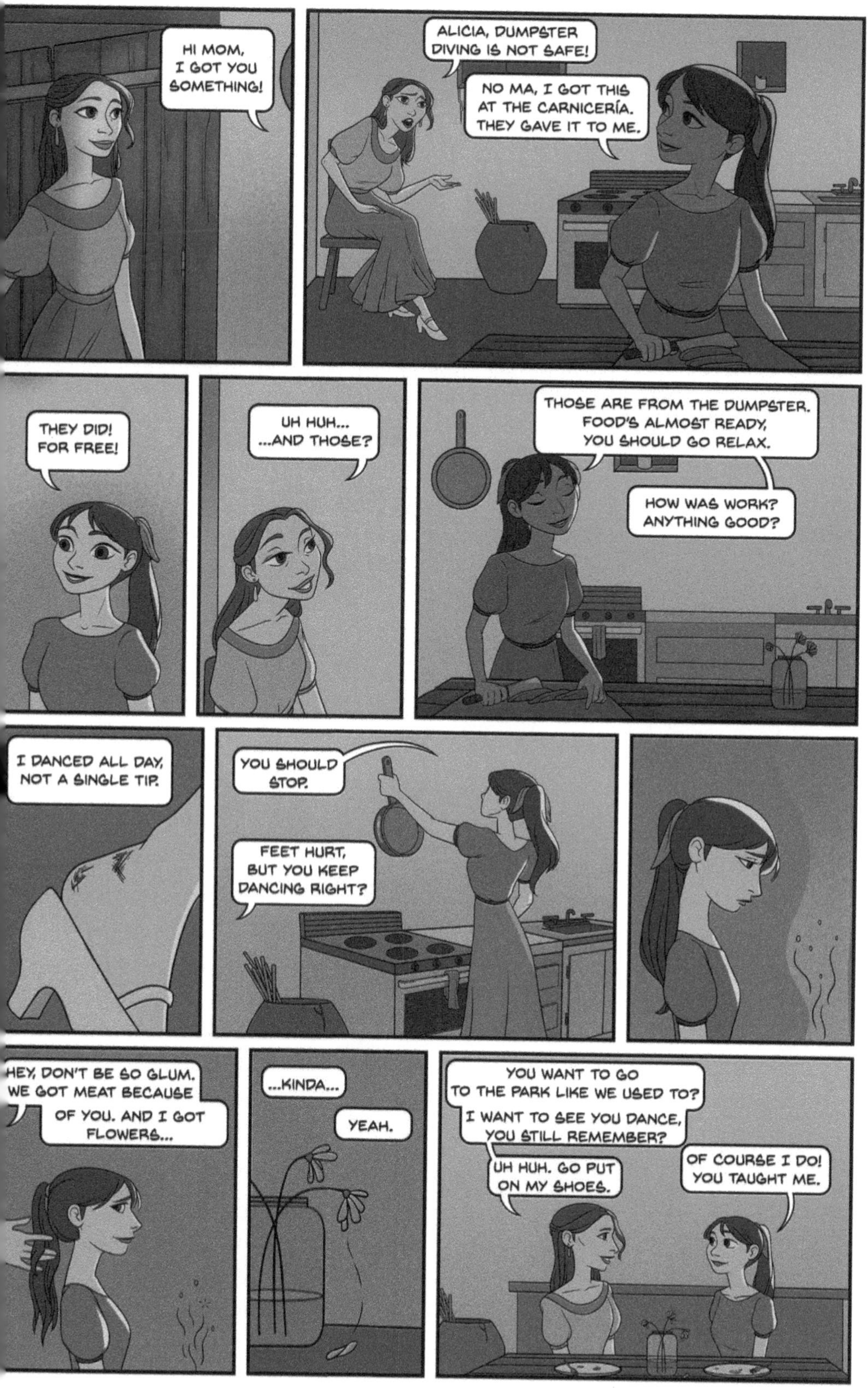
HI MOM, I GOT YOU SOMETHING!
ALICIA, DUMPSTER DIVING IS NOT SAFE!
NO MA, I GOT THIS AT THE CARNICERÍA. THEY GAVE IT TO ME.
THEY DID! FOR FREE!
UH HUH... ...AND THOSE?
THOSE ARE FROM THE DUMPSTER. FOOD'S ALMOST READY, YOU SHOULD GO RELAX.
HOW WAS WORK? ANYTHING GOOD?
I DANCED ALL DAY, NOT A SINGLE TIP.
YOU SHOULD STOP.
FEET HURT, BUT YOU KEEP DANCING RIGHT?
HEY, DON'T BE SO GLUM. WE GOT MEAT BECAUSE
OF YOU. AND I GOT FLOWERS...
...KINDA...
YEAH.
YOU WANT TO GO TO THE PARK LIKE WE USED TO?
I WANT TO SEE YOU DANCE, YOU STILL REMEMBER?
OF COURSE I DO! YOU TAUGHT ME.
UH HUH. GO PUT ON MY SHOES.

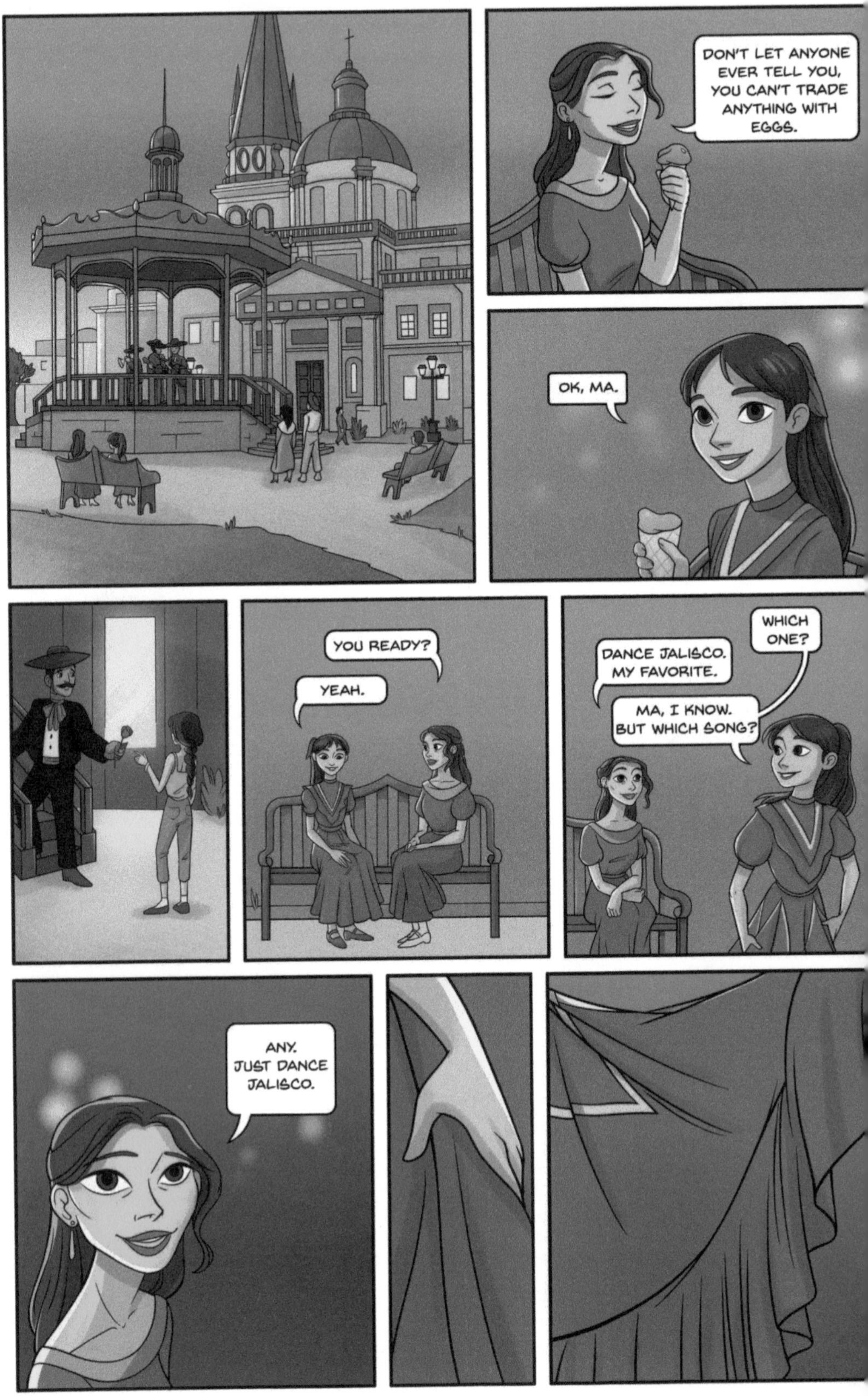
DON'T LET ANYONE EVER TELL YOU, YOU CAN'T TRADE ANYTHING WITH EGGS.
OK, MA.
YOU READY?
YEAH.
DANCE JALISCO. MY FAVORITE.
WHICH ONE?
MA, I KNOW. BUT WHICH SONG?
ANY. JUST DANCE JALISCO.

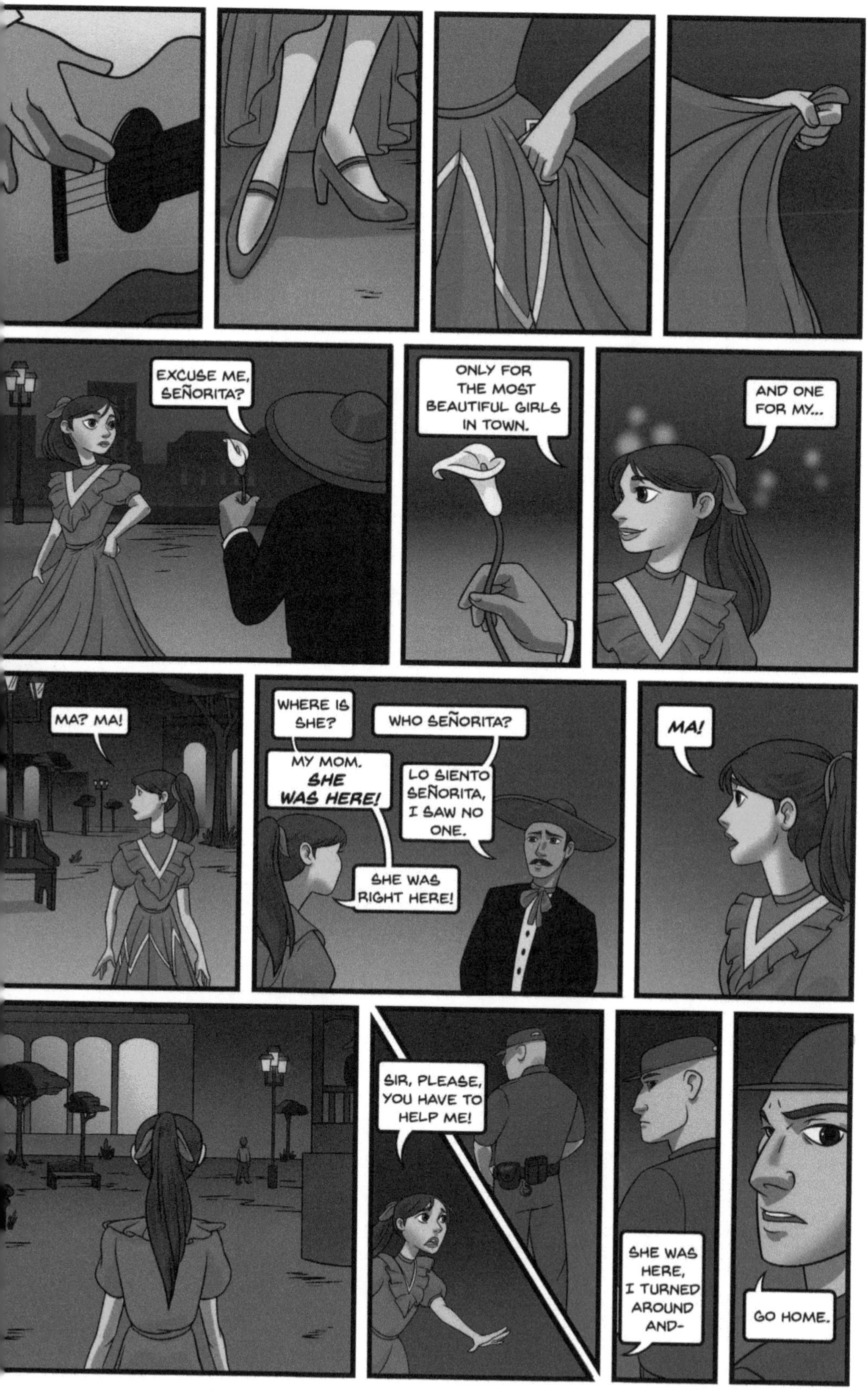
EXCUSE ME, SEÑORITA?
ONLY FOR THE MOST BEAUTIFUL GIRLS IN TOWN.
AND ONE FOR MY...
MA? MA!
WHERE IS SHE?
WHO SEÑORITA?
MY MOM. SHE WAS HERE!
LO SIENTO SEÑORITA, I SAW NO ONE.
SHE WAS RIGHT HERE!
MA!
SIR, PLEASE, YOU HAVE TO HELP ME!
SHE WAS HERE, I TURNED AROUND AND-
GO HOME.

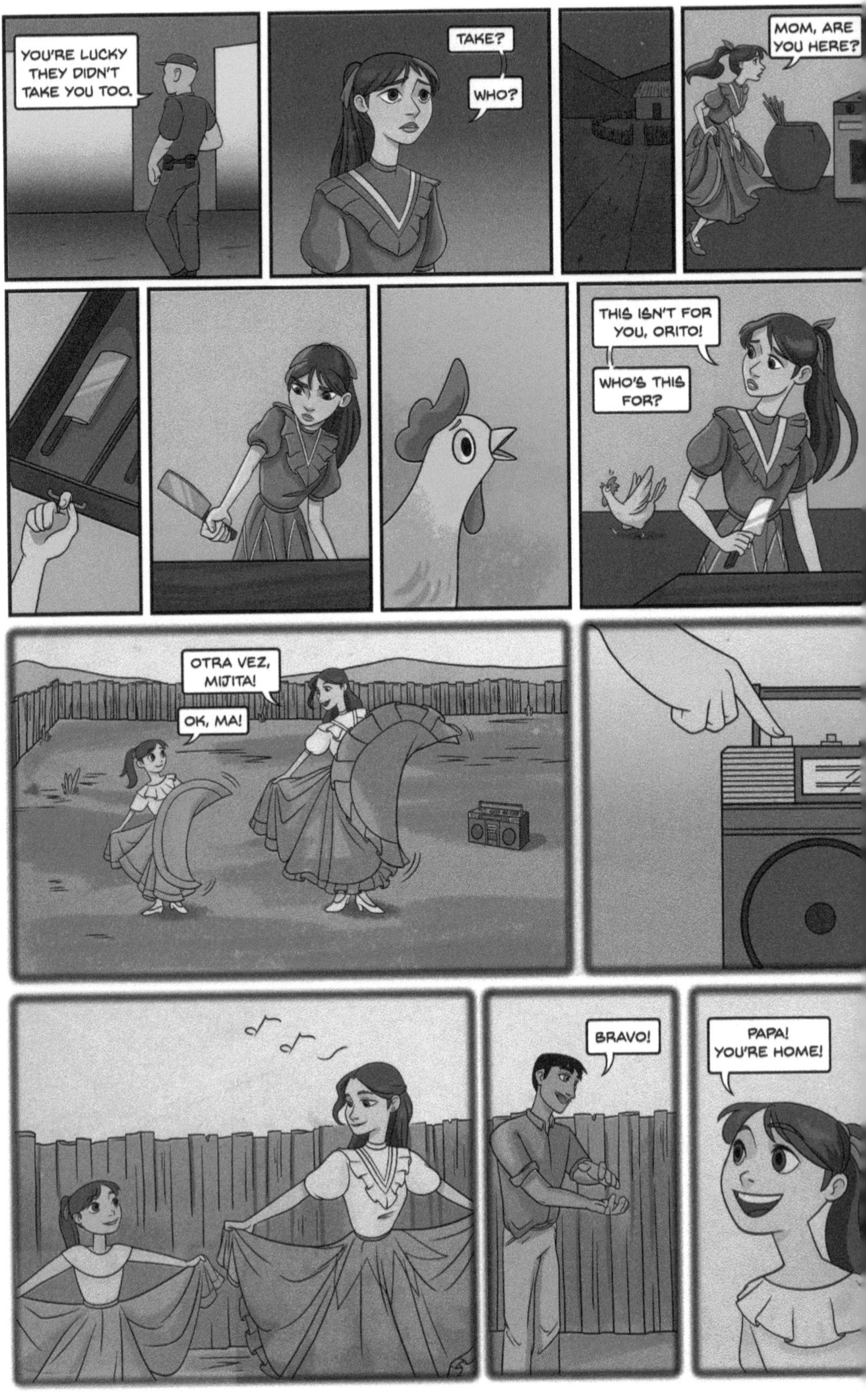
YOU'RE LUCKY THEY DIDN'T TAKE YOU TOO.
TAKE?
WHO?
MOM, ARE YOU HERE?
THIS ISN'T FOR YOU, ORITO!
WHO'S THIS FOR?
OTRA VEZ, MIJITA!
OK, MA!
BRAVO!
PAPA! YOU'RE HOME!

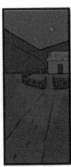

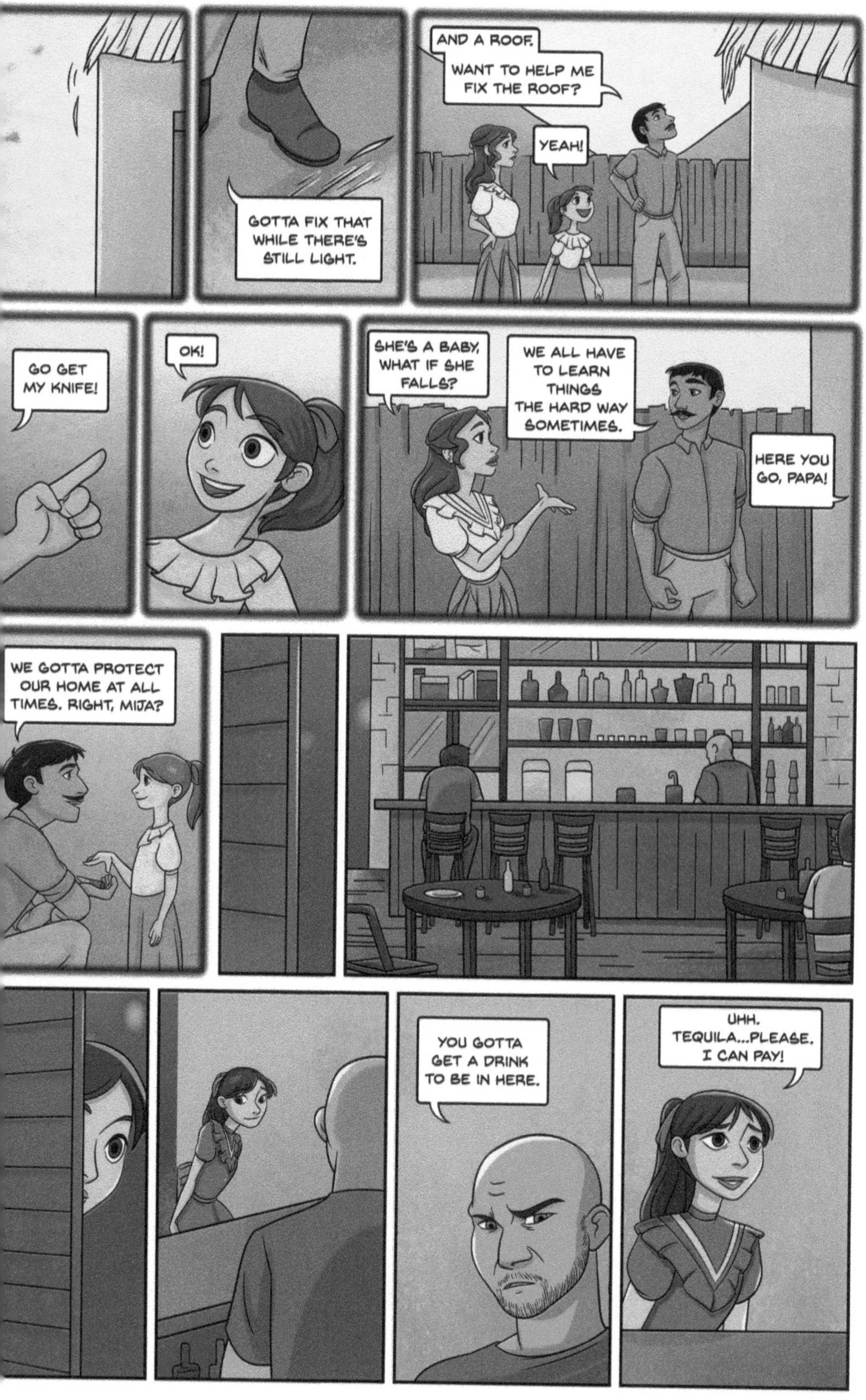
GOTTA FIX THAT WHILE THERE'S STILL LIGHT.
AND A ROOF.
WANT TO HELP ME FIX THE ROOF?
YEAH!
GO GET MY KNIFE!
OK!
SHE'S A BABY, WHAT IF SHE FALLS?
WE ALL HAVE TO LEARN THINGS THE HARD WAY SOMETIMES.
HERE YOU GO, PAPA!
WE GOTTA PROTECT OUR HOME AT ALL TIMES. RIGHT, MIJA?
YOU GOTTA GET A DRINK TO BE IN HERE.
UHH. TEQUILA...PLEASE. I CAN PAY!

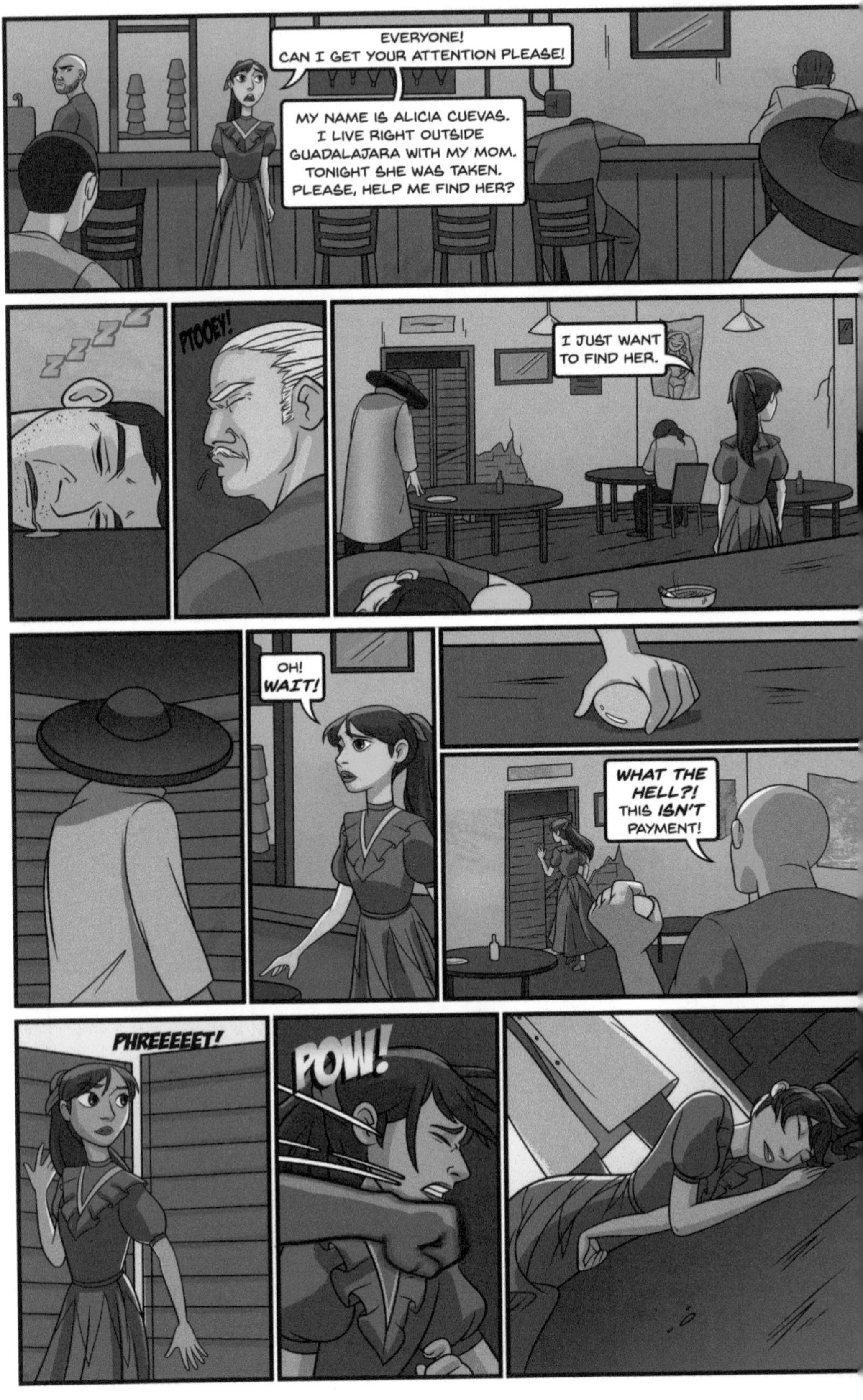
EVERYONE!
CAN I GET YOUR ATTENTION PLEASE!
MY NAME IS ALICIA CUEVAS. I LIVE RIGHT OUTSIDE GUADALAJARA WITH MY MOM. TONIGHT SHE WAS TAKEN. PLEASE, HELP ME FIND HER?
PTOOEY!
I JUST WANT TO FIND HER.
OH! WAIT!
WHAT THE HELL?! THIS ISN'T PAYMENT!
PHREEEEET!
POW!

CHAPTER 2

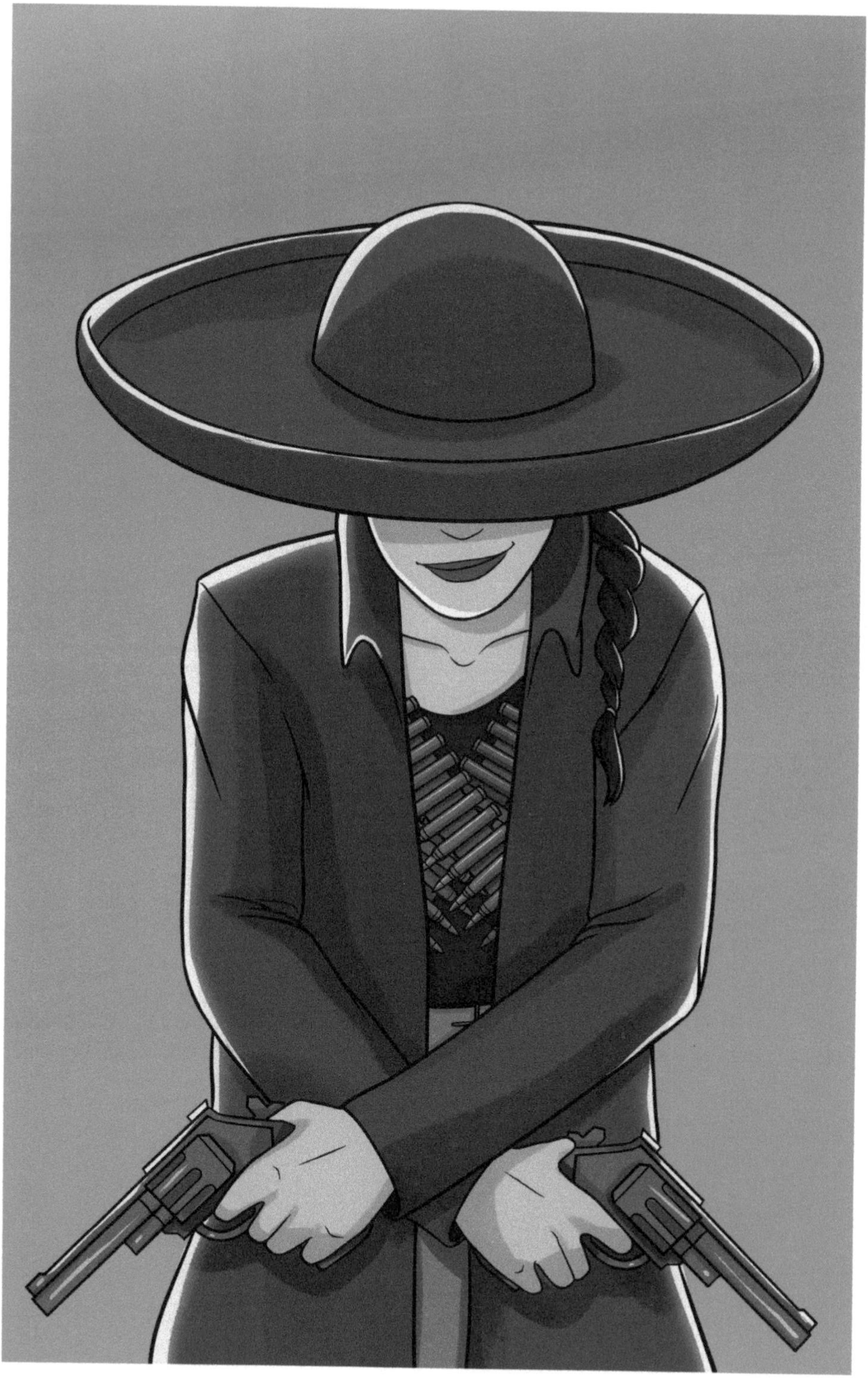

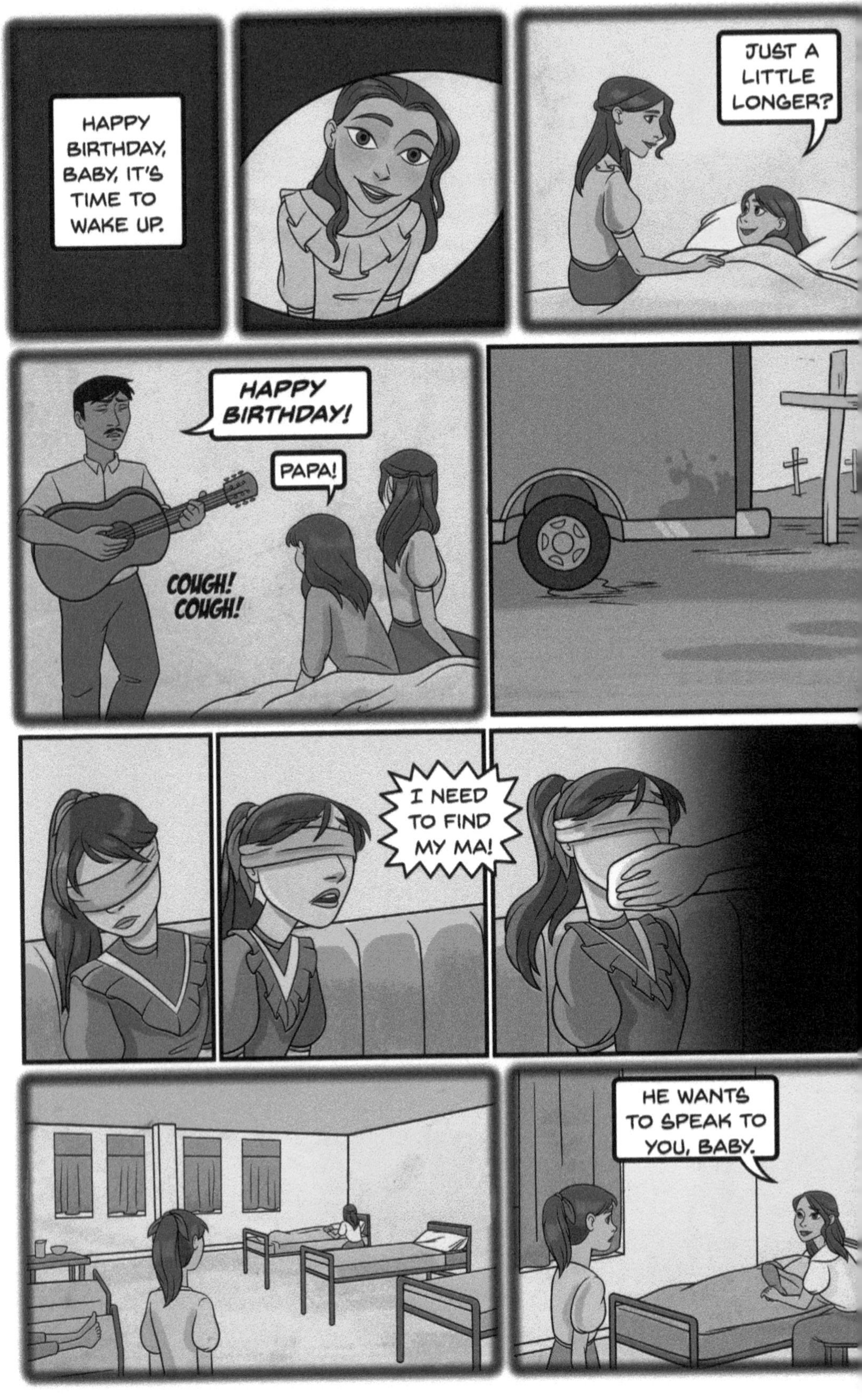
HAPPY BIRTHDAY, BABY, IT'S TIME TO WAKE UP.
JUST A LITTLE LONGER?
HAPPY BIRTHDAY!
PAPA!
COUGH! COUGH!
I NEED TO FIND MY MA!
HE WANTS TO SPEAK TO YOU, BABY.

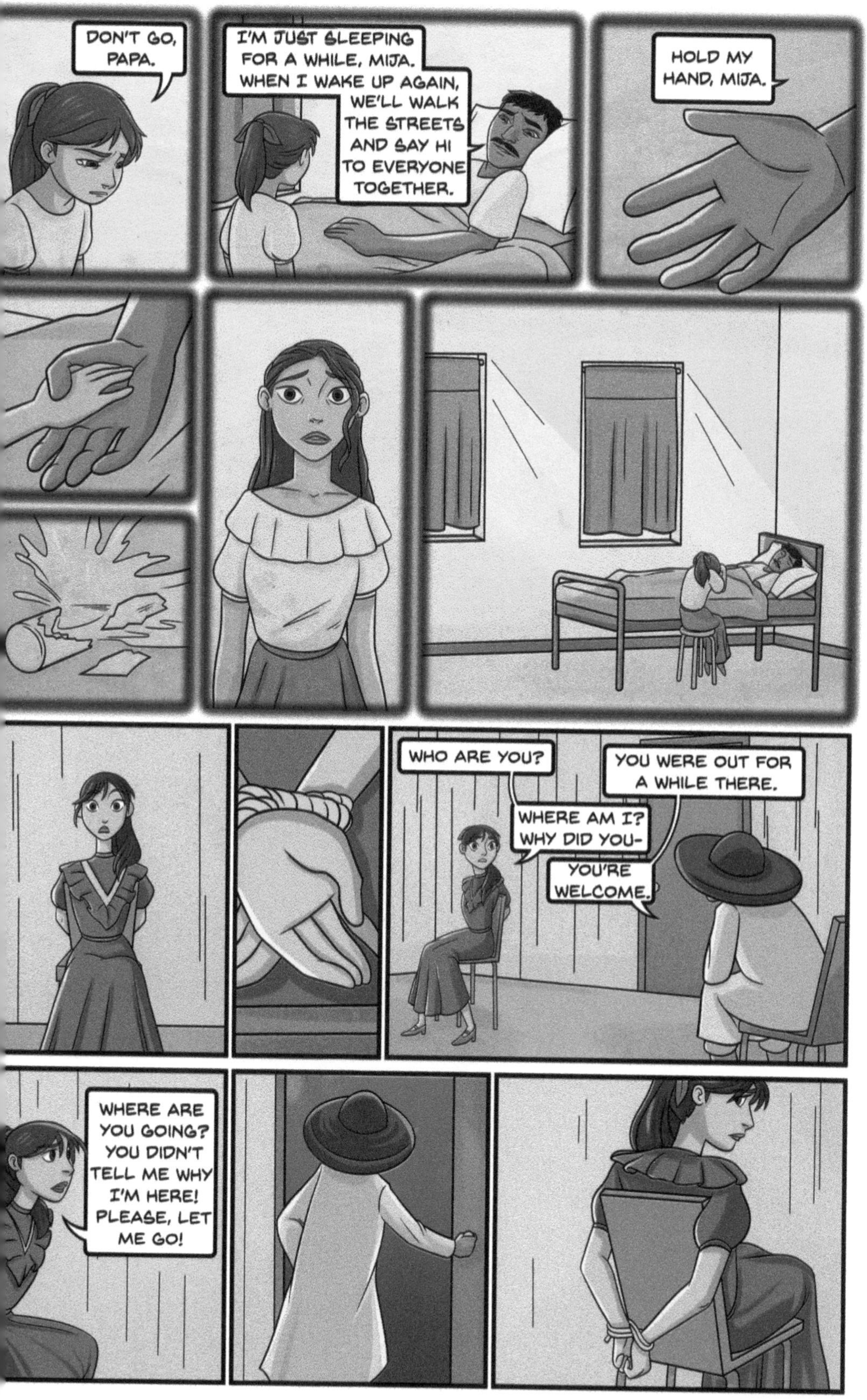
DON'T GO, PAPA.
I'M JUST SLEEPING FOR A WHILE, MIJA. WHEN I WAKE UP AGAIN, WE'LL WALK THE STREETS AND SAY HI TO EVERYONE TOGETHER.
HOLD MY HAND, MIJA.
WHO ARE YOU?
WHERE AM I? WHY DID YOU-
YOU WERE OUT FOR A WHILE THERE.
YOU'RE WELCOME.
WHERE ARE YOU GOING? YOU DIDN'T TELL ME WHY I'M HERE! PLEASE, LET ME GO!

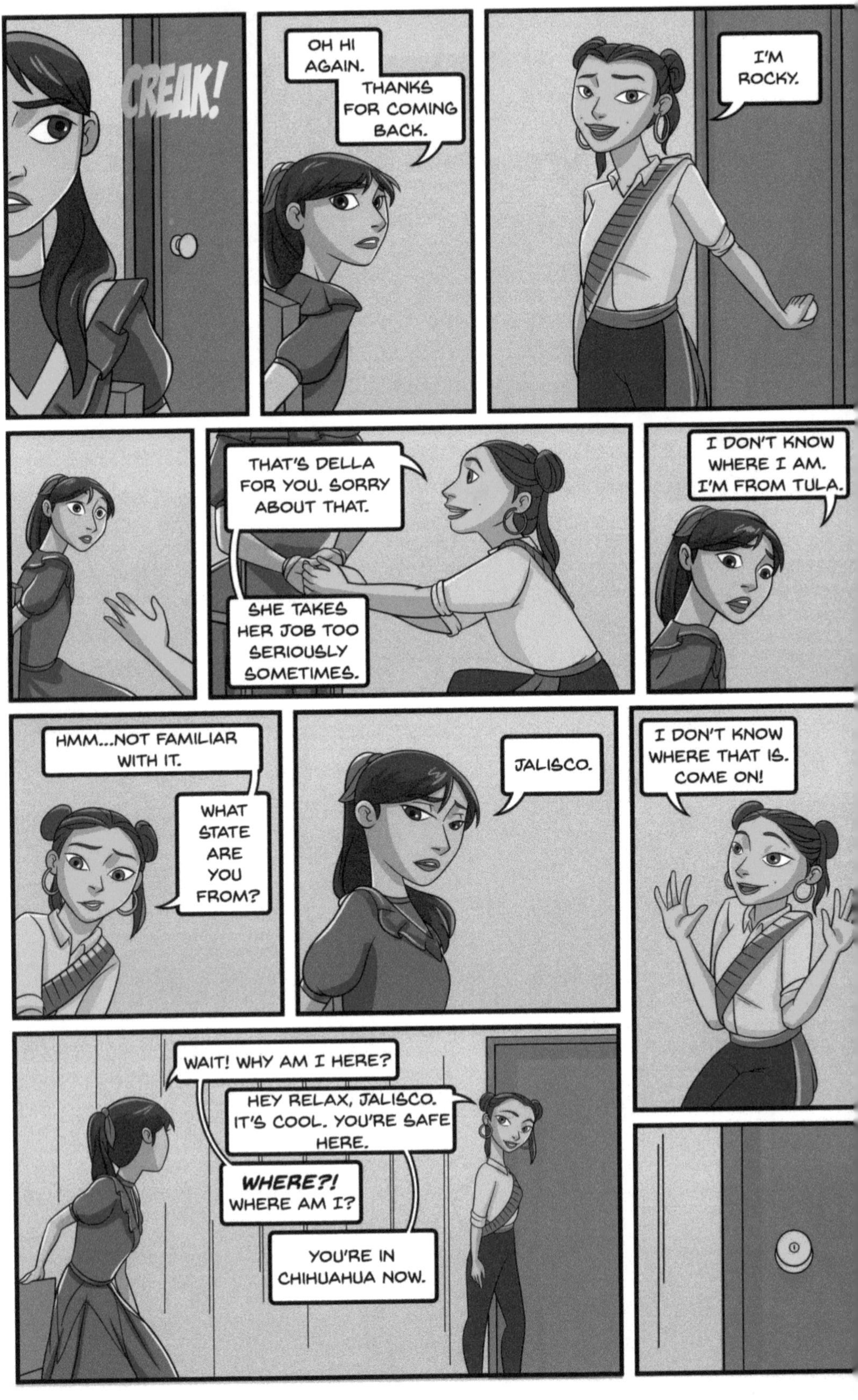
CREAK!
OH HI AGAIN.
THANKS FOR COMING BACK.
I'M ROCKY.
THAT'S DELLA FOR YOU. SORRY ABOUT THAT.
SHE TAKES HER JOB TOO SERIOUSLY SOMETIMES.
I DON'T KNOW WHERE I AM. I'M FROM TULA.
HMM...NOT FAMILIAR WITH IT.
WHAT STATE ARE YOU FROM?
JALISCO.
I DON'T KNOW WHERE THAT IS. COME ON!
WAIT! WHY AM I HERE?
HEY RELAX, JALISCO. IT'S COOL. YOU'RE SAFE HERE.
WHERE?! WHERE AM I?
YOU'RE IN CHIHUAHUA NOW.

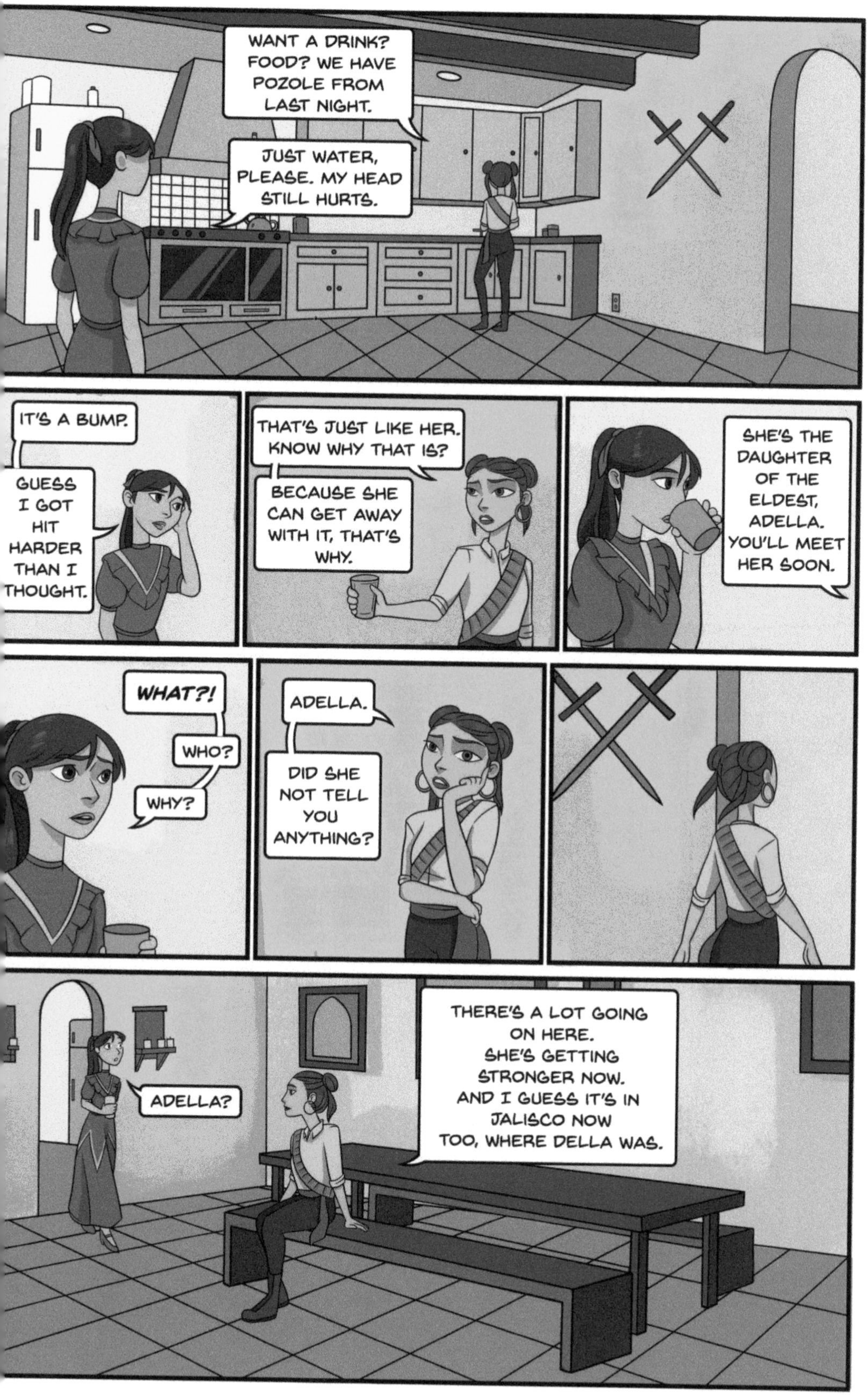

WANT A DRINK? FOOD? WE HAVE POZOLE FROM LAST NIGHT.
JUST WATER, PLEASE. MY HEAD STILL HURTS.
IT'S A BUMP.
GUESS I GOT HIT HARDER THAN I THOUGHT.
THAT'S JUST LIKE HER. KNOW WHY THAT IS?
BECAUSE SHE CAN GET AWAY WITH IT, THAT'S WHY.
SHE'S THE DAUGHTER OF THE ELDEST, ADELLA. YOU'LL MEET HER SOON.
WHAT?!
WHO?
WHY?
ADELLA.
DID SHE NOT TELL YOU ANYTHING?
ADELLA?
THERE'S A LOT GOING ON HERE. SHE'S GETTING STRONGER NOW. AND I GUESS IT'S IN JALISCO NOW TOO, WHERE DELLA WAS.

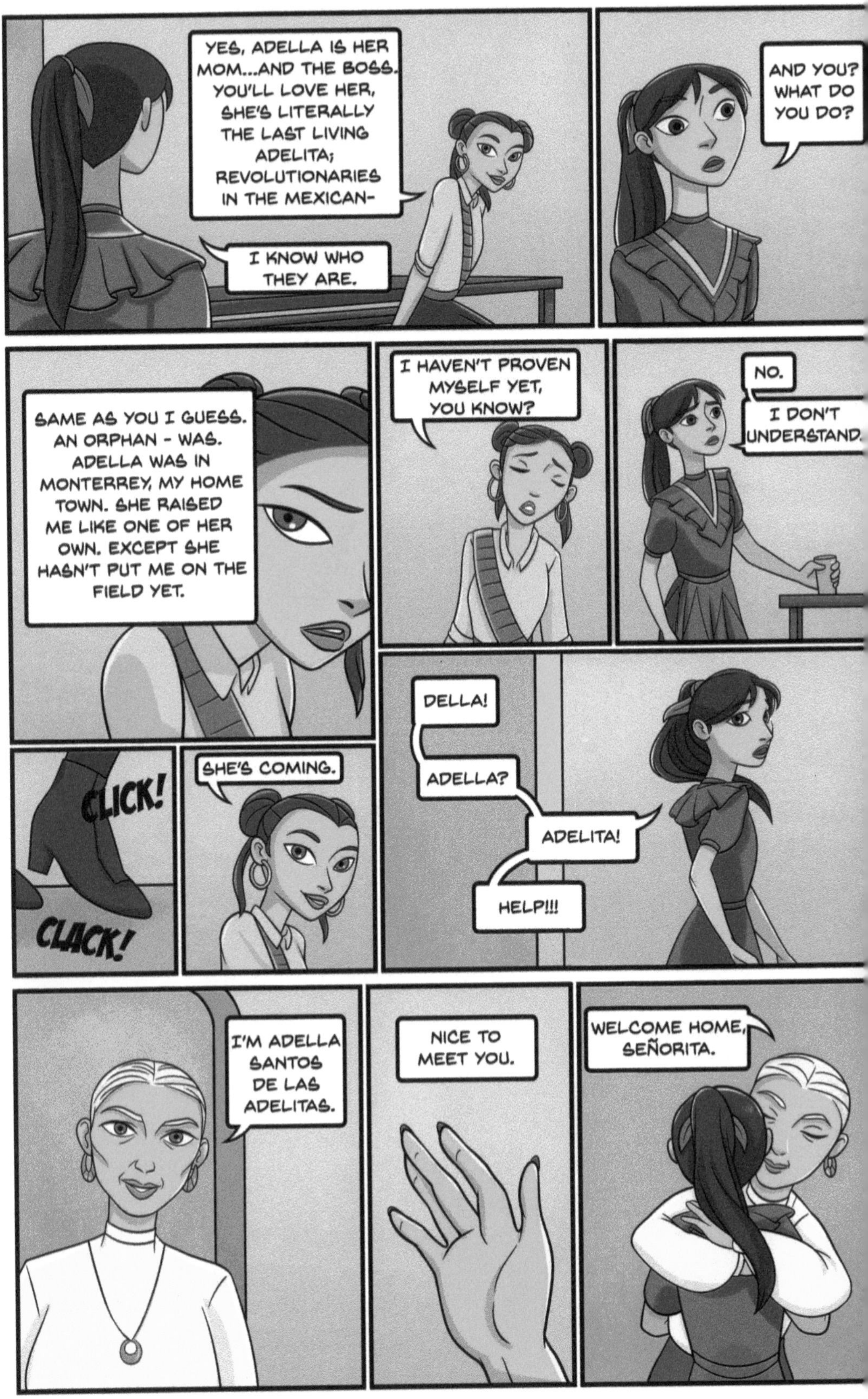
YES, ADELLA IS HER MOM...AND THE BOSS. YOU'LL LOVE HER, SHE'S LITERALLY THE LAST LIVING ADELITA; REVOLUTIONARIES IN THE MEXICAN-
I KNOW WHO THEY ARE.
AND YOU? WHAT DO YOU DO?
SAME AS YOU I GUESS. AN ORPHAN - WAS. ADELLA WAS IN MONTERREY, MY HOME TOWN. SHE RAISED ME LIKE ONE OF HER OWN. EXCEPT SHE HASN'T PUT ME ON THE FIELD YET.
I HAVEN'T PROVEN MYSELF YET, YOU KNOW?
NO.
I DON'T UNDERSTAND.
CLICK!
CLACK!
SHE'S COMING.
DELLA!
ADELLA?
ADELITA!
HELP!!!
I'M ADELLA SANTOS DE LAS ADELITAS.
NICE TO MEET YOU.
WELCOME HOME, SEÑORITA.

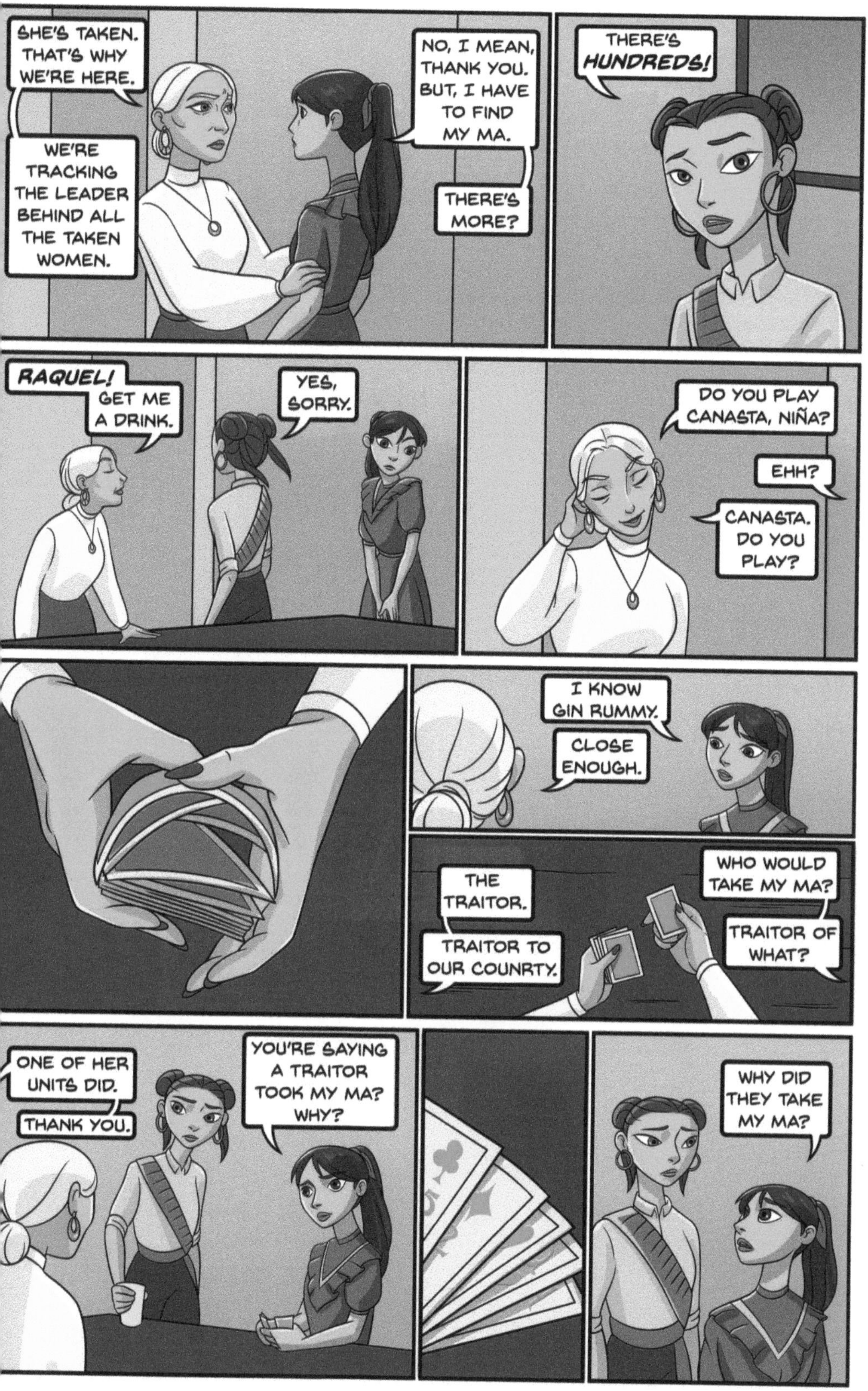
SHE'S TAKEN. THAT'S WHY WE'RE HERE.
WE'RE TRACKING THE LEADER BEHIND ALL THE TAKEN WOMEN.
NO, I MEAN, THANK YOU. BUT, I HAVE TO FIND MY MA.
THERE'S MORE?
THERE'S HUNDREDS!
RAQUEL! GET ME A DRINK.
YES, SORRY.
DO YOU PLAY CANASTA, NIÑA?
EHH?
CANASTA. DO YOU PLAY?
I KNOW GIN RUMMY.
CLOSE ENOUGH.
WHO WOULD TAKE MY MA?
THE TRAITOR.
TRAITOR OF WHAT?
TRAITOR TO OUR COUNRTY.
ONE OF HER UNITS DID.
THANK YOU.
YOU'RE SAYING A TRAITOR TOOK MY MA? WHY?
WHY DID THEY TAKE MY MA?

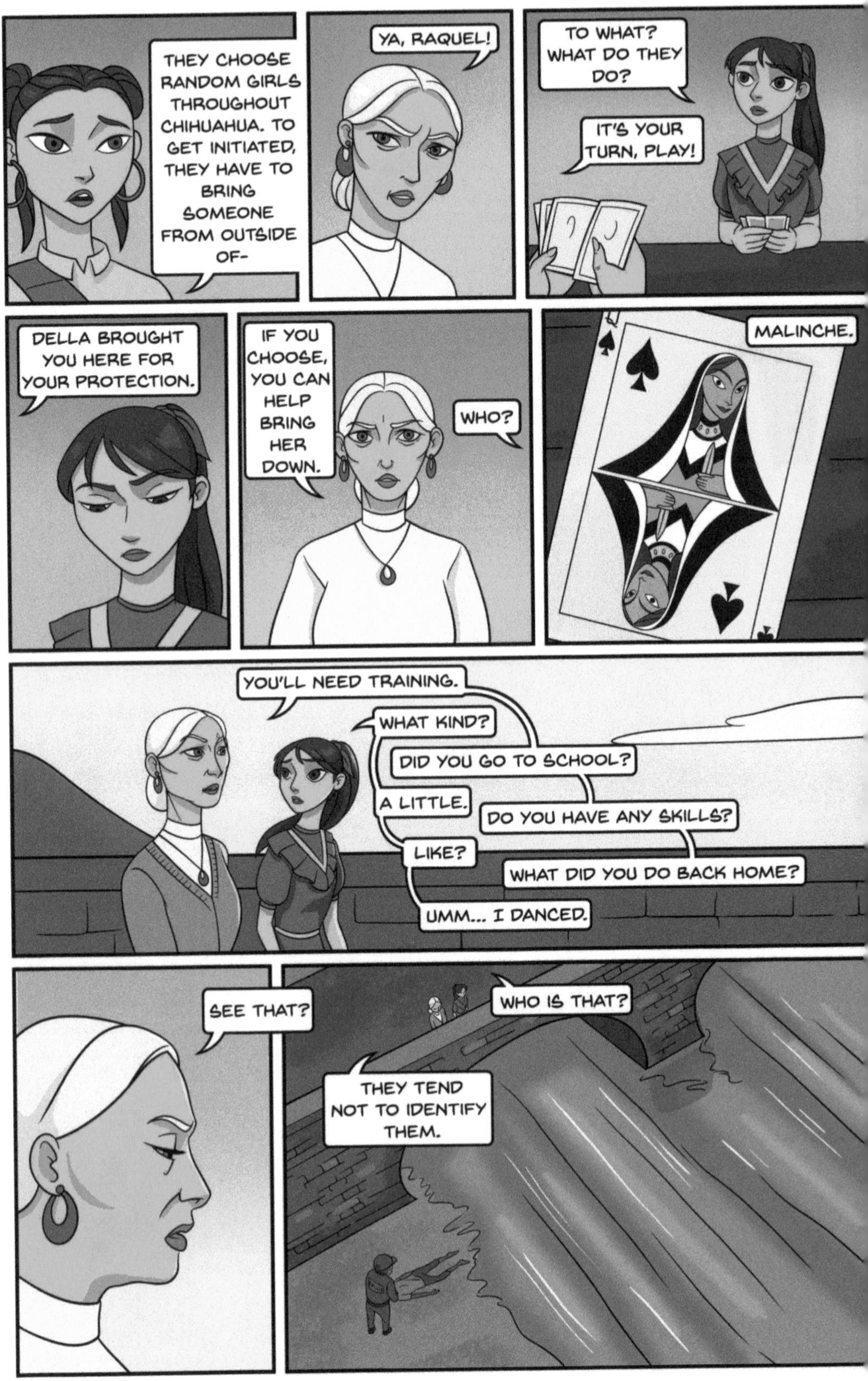
THEY CHOOSE RANDOM GIRLS THROUGHOUT CHIHUAHUA. TO GET INITIATED, THEY HAVE TO BRING SOMEONE FROM OUTSIDE OF-
YA, RAQUEL!
TO WHAT? WHAT DO THEY DO?
IT'S YOUR TURN, PLAY!
DELLA BROUGHT YOU HERE FOR YOUR PROTECTION.
IF YOU CHOOSE, YOU CAN HELP BRING HER DOWN.
WHO?
MALINCHE.
YOU'LL NEED TRAINING.
WHAT KIND?
DID YOU GO TO SCHOOL?
A LITTLE.
DO YOU HAVE ANY SKILLS?
LIKE?
WHAT DID YOU DO BACK HOME?
UMM... I DANCED.
SEE THAT?
WHO IS THAT?
THEY TEND NOT TO IDENTIFY THEM.

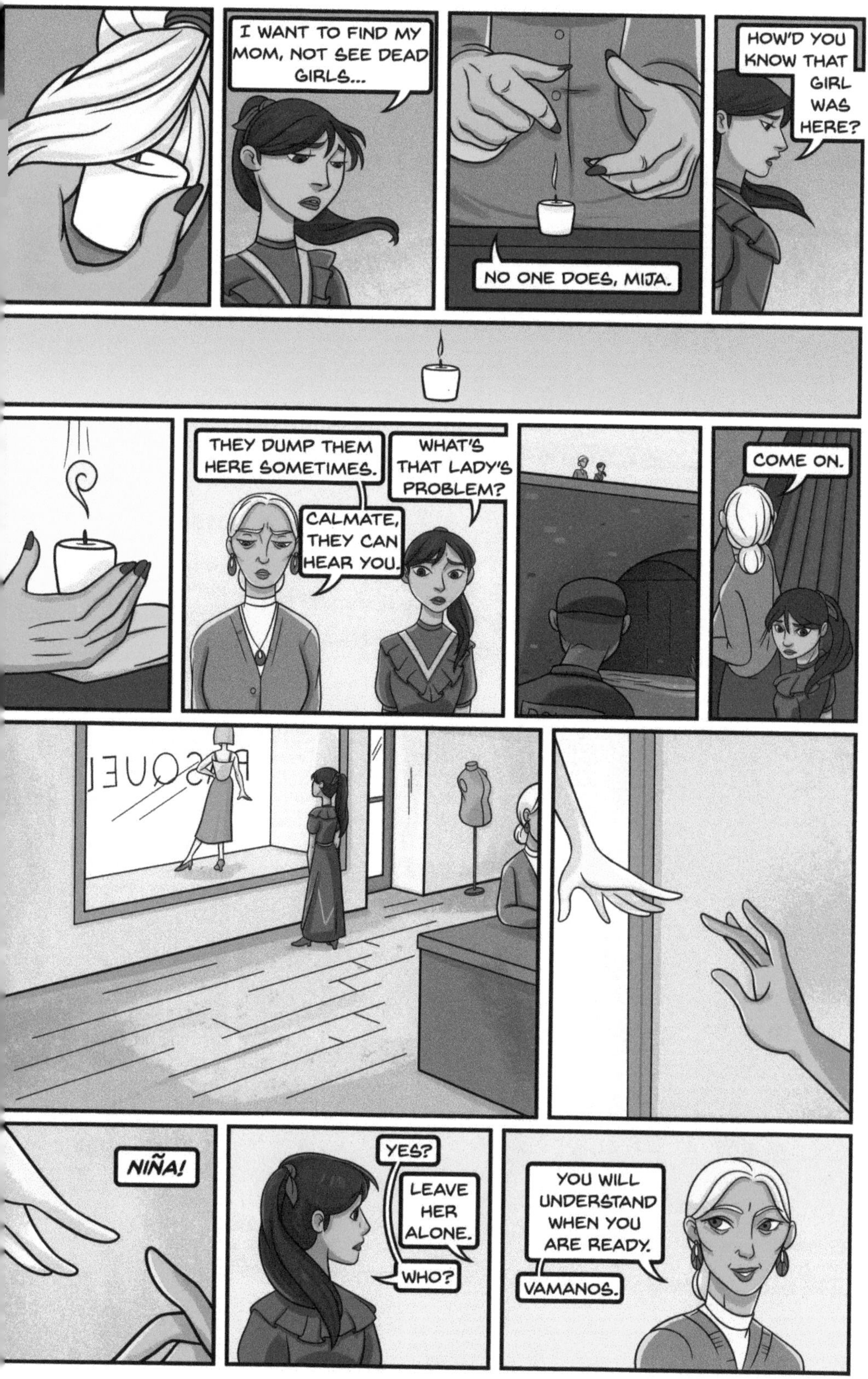
I WANT TO FIND MY MOM, NOT SEE DEAD GIRLS...
NO ONE DOES, MIJA.
HOW'D YOU KNOW THAT GIRL WAS HERE?
THEY DUMP THEM HERE SOMETIMES.
WHAT'S THAT LADY'S PROBLEM?
CALMATE, THEY CAN HEAR YOU.
COME ON.
NIÑA!
YES?
LEAVE HER ALONE.
WHO?
YOU WILL UNDERSTAND WHEN YOU ARE READY.
VAMANOS.

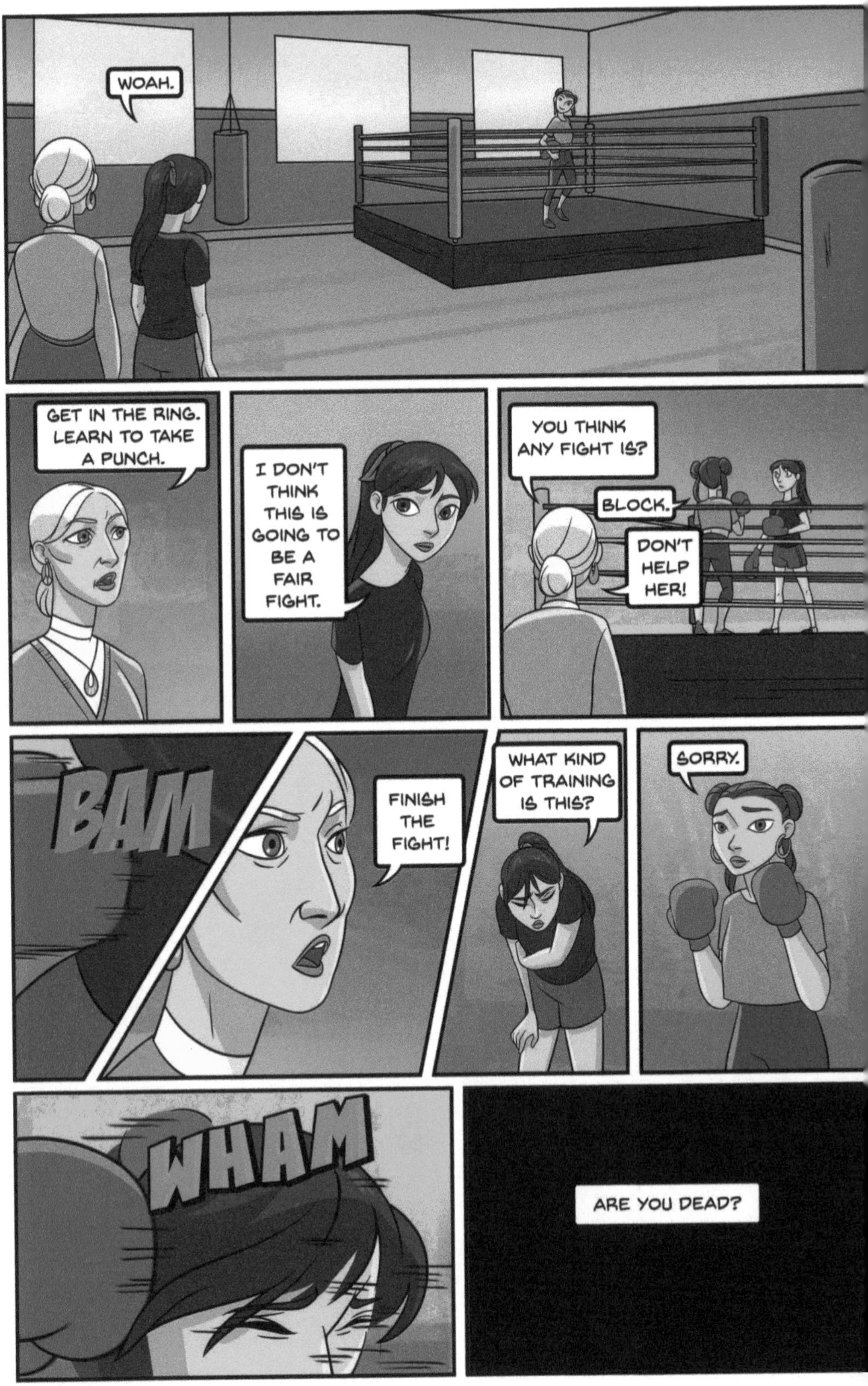
WOAH.
GET IN THE RING. LEARN TO TAKE A PUNCH.
I DON'T THINK THIS IS GOING TO BE A FAIR FIGHT.
YOU THINK ANY FIGHT IS?
BLOCK.
DON'T HELP HER!
BAM
FINISH THE FIGHT!
WHAT KIND OF TRAINING IS THIS?
SORRY.
WHAM
ARE YOU DEAD?

CHAPTER 3

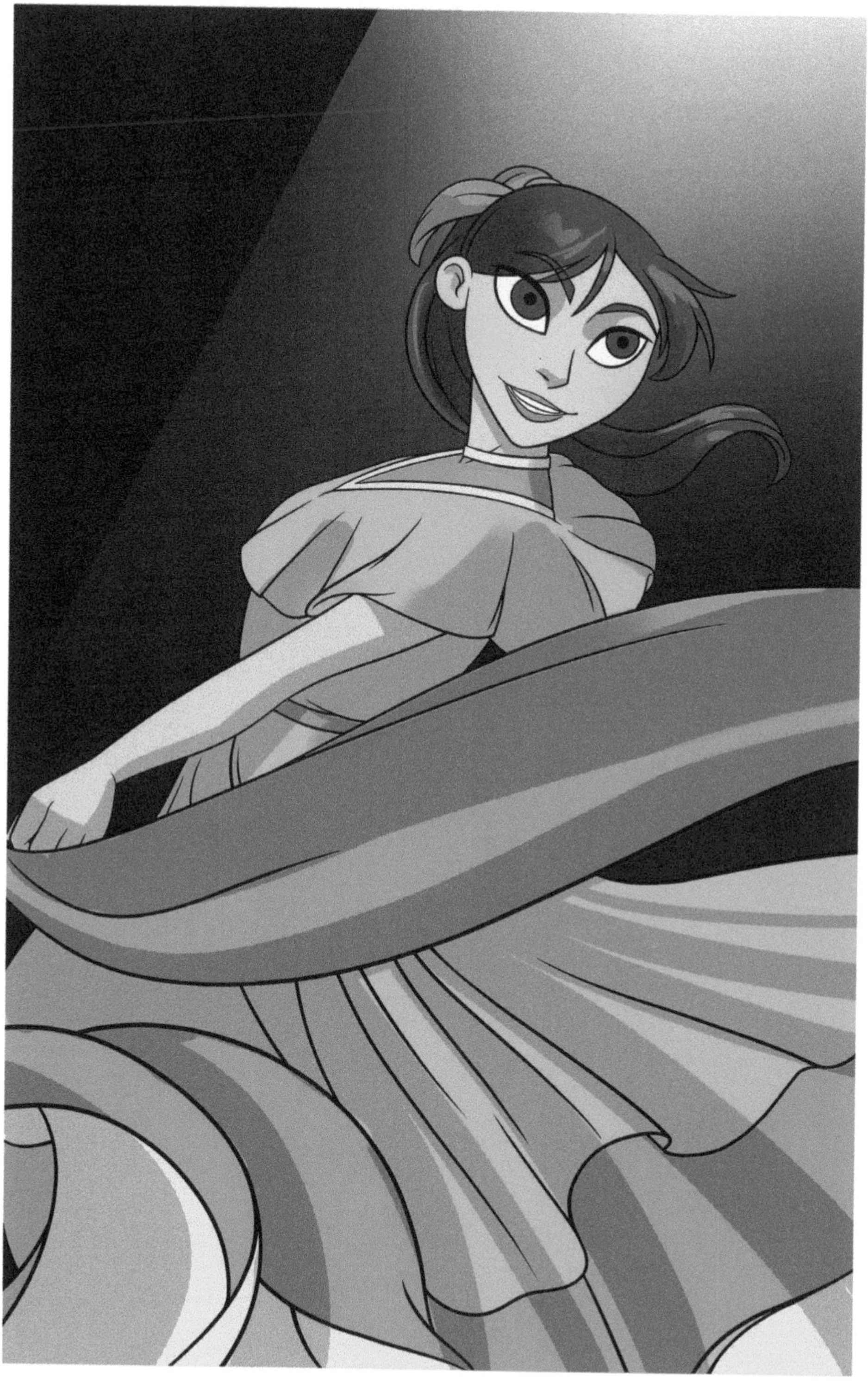

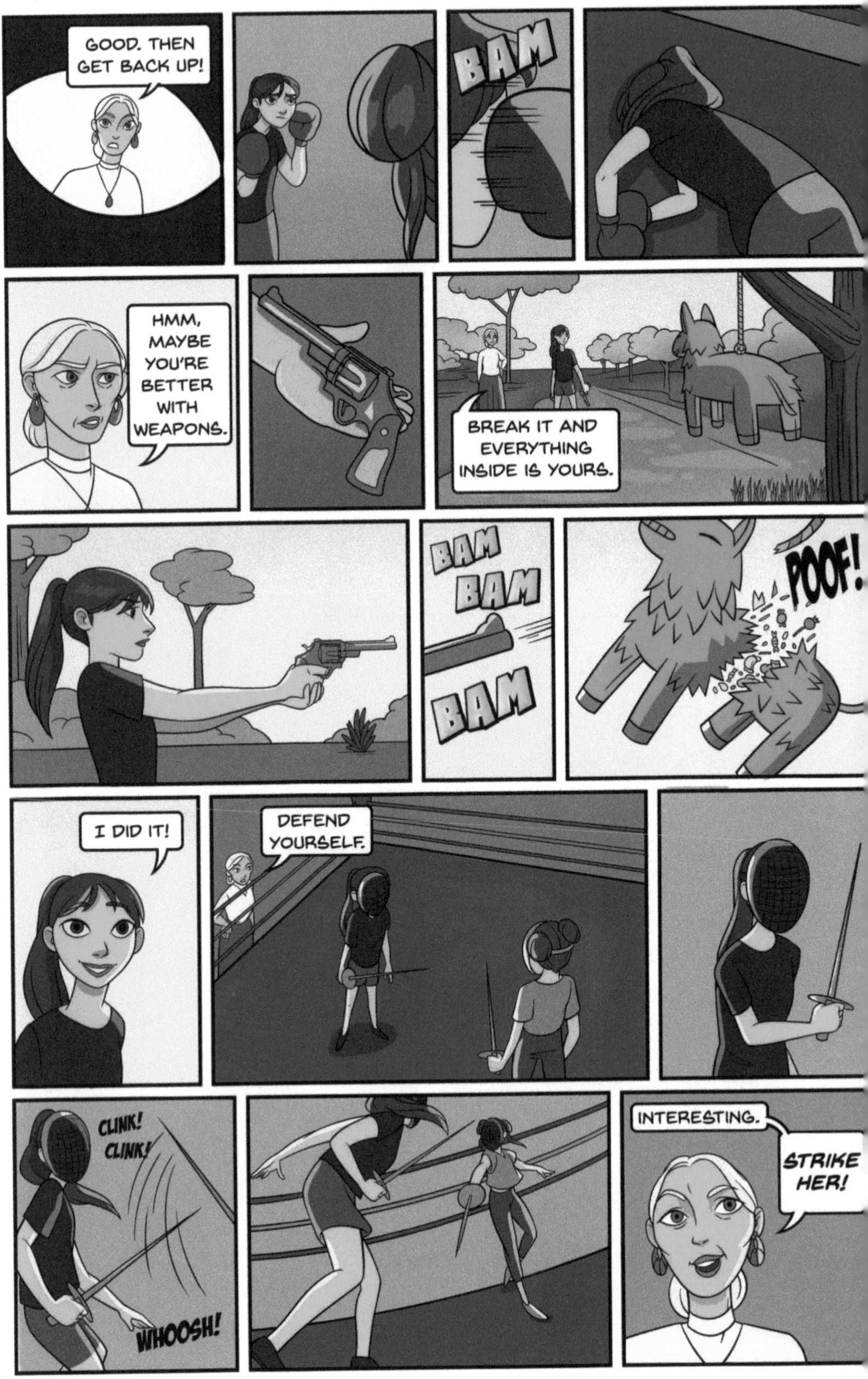
GOOD. THEN GET BACK UP!
BAM
HMM, MAYBE YOU'RE BETTER WITH WEAPONS.
BREAK IT AND EVERYTHING INSIDE IS YOURS.
BAM
BAM
BAM
POOF!
I DID IT!
DEFEND YOURSELF.
CLINK!
CLINK!
WHOOSH!
INTERESTING.
STRIKE HER!

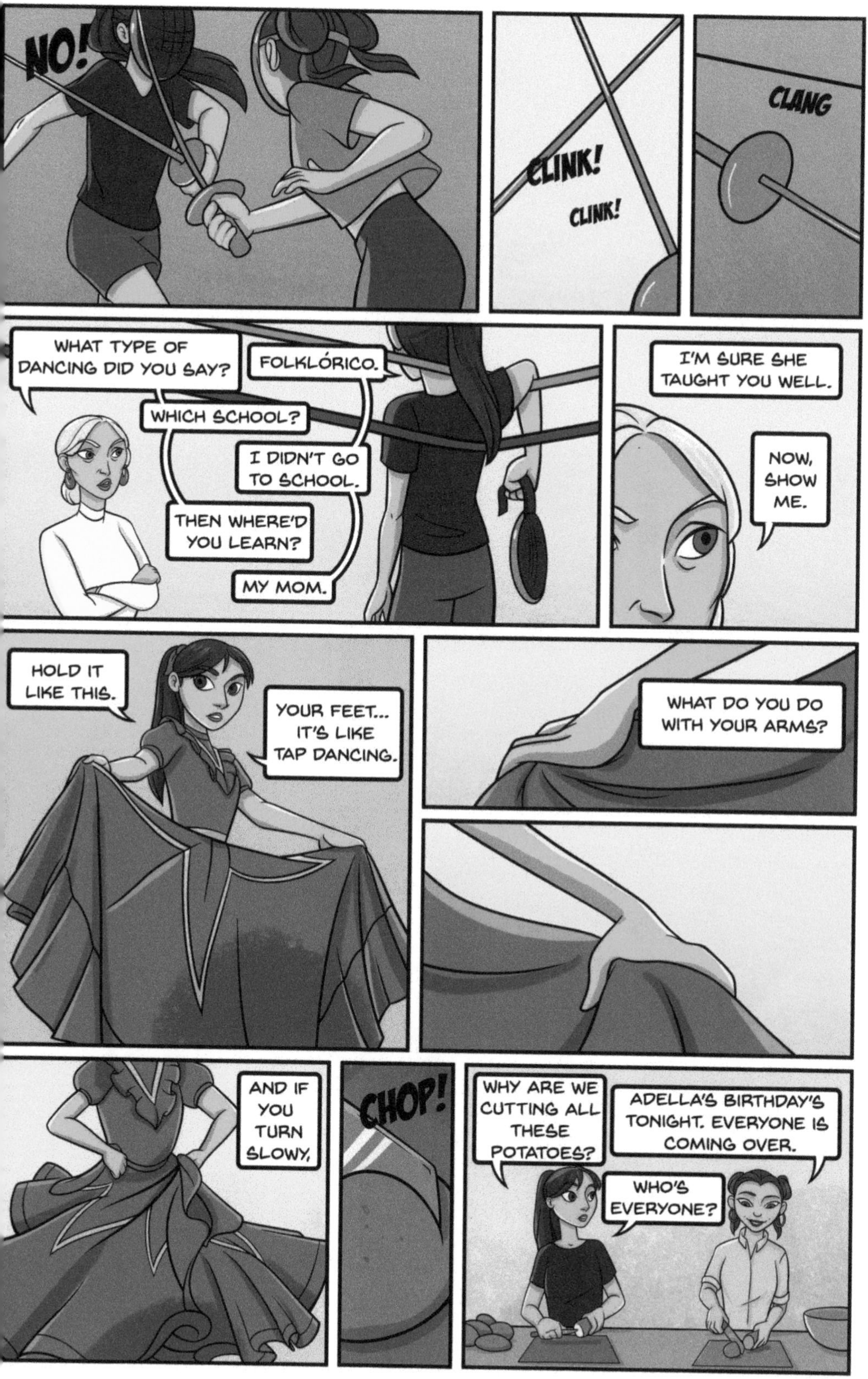
NO!
CLINK!
CLINK!
CLANG
WHAT TYPE OF DANCING DID YOU SAY?
FOLKLÓRICO.
WHICH SCHOOL?
I DIDN'T GO TO SCHOOL.
THEN WHERE'D YOU LEARN?
MY MOM.
I'M SURE SHE TAUGHT YOU WELL.
NOW, SHOW ME.
HOLD IT LIKE THIS.
YOUR FEET... IT'S LIKE TAP DANCING.
WHAT DO YOU DO WITH YOUR ARMS?
AND IF YOU TURN SLOWY,
CHOP!
WHY ARE WE CUTTING ALL THESE POTATOES?
ADELLA'S BIRTHDAY'S TONIGHT. EVERYONE IS COMING OVER.
WHO'S EVERYONE?

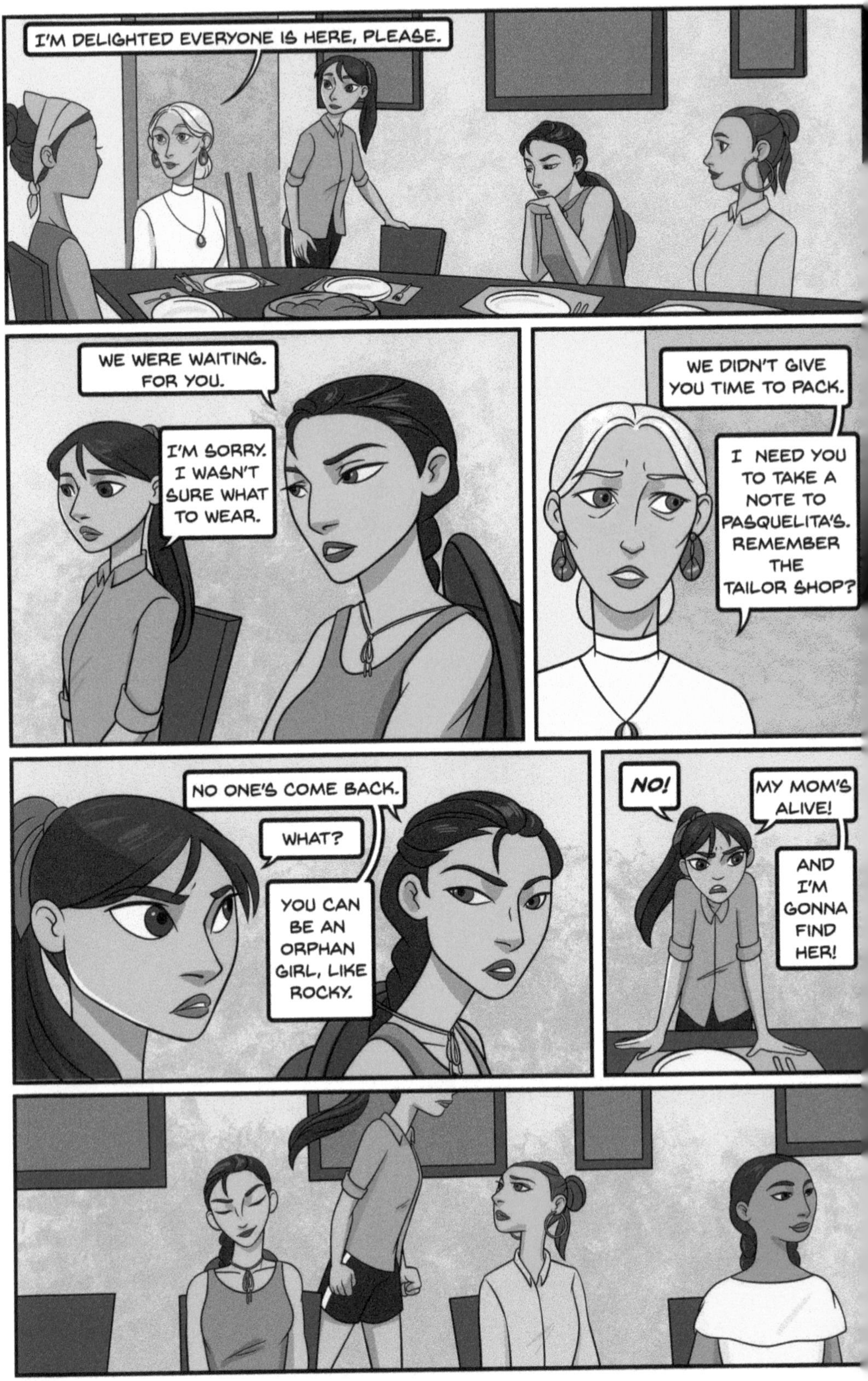
I'M DELIGHTED EVERYONE IS HERE, PLEASE.
WE WERE WAITING. FOR YOU.
I'M SORRY. I WASN'T SURE WHAT TO WEAR.
WE DIDN'T GIVE YOU TIME TO PACK.
I NEED YOU TO TAKE A NOTE TO PASQUELITA'S. REMEMBER THE TAILOR SHOP?
NO ONE'S COME BACK.
WHAT?
YOU CAN BE AN ORPHAN GIRL, LIKE ROCKY.
NO!
MY MOM'S ALIVE!
AND I'M GONNA FIND HER!

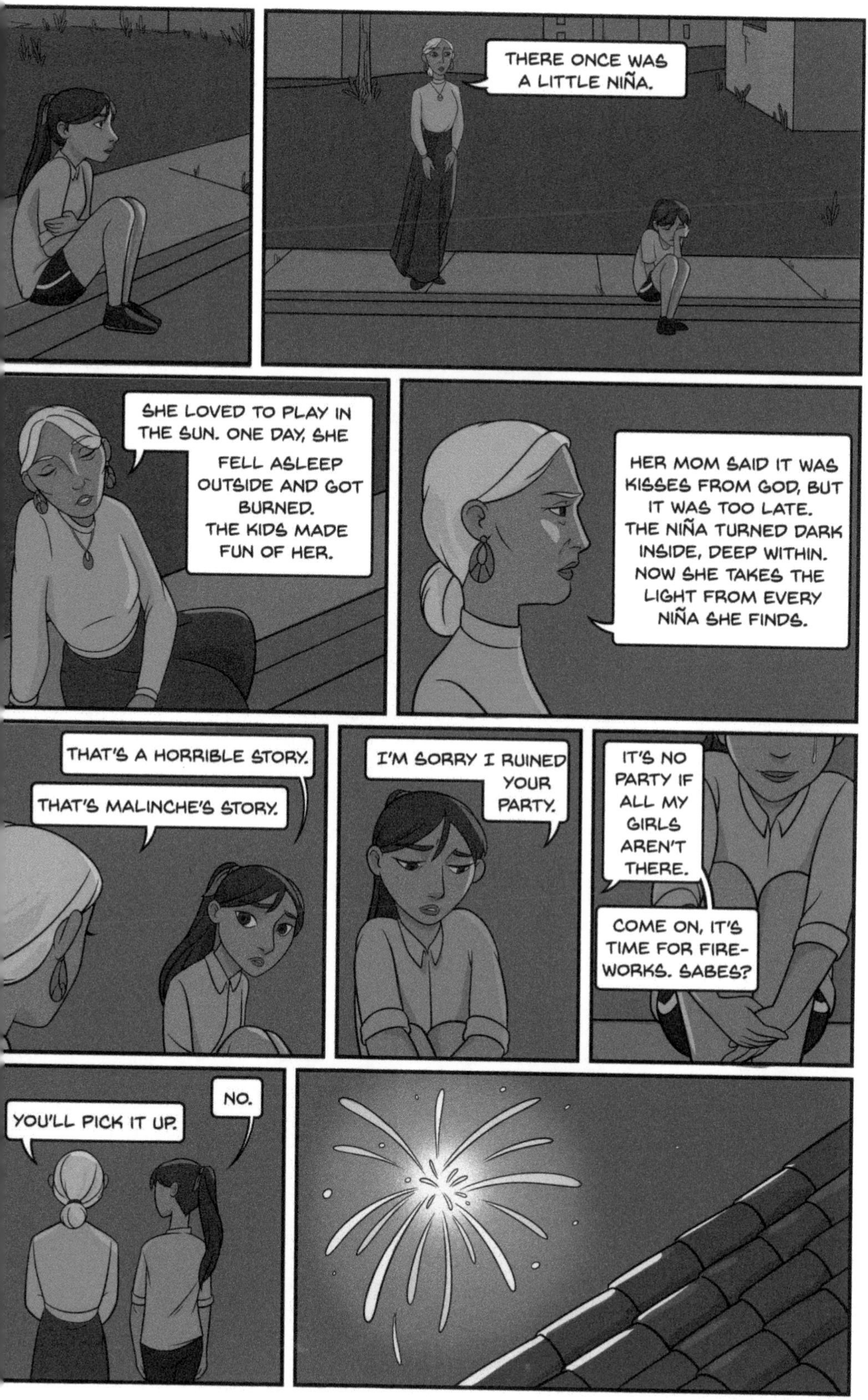
THERE ONCE WAS A LITTLE NIÑA.
SHE LOVED TO PLAY IN THE SUN. ONE DAY, SHE FELL ASLEEP OUTSIDE AND GOT BURNED. THE KIDS MADE FUN OF HER.
HER MOM SAID IT WAS KISSES FROM GOD, BUT IT WAS TOO LATE. THE NIÑA TURNED DARK INSIDE, DEEP WITHIN. NOW SHE TAKES THE LIGHT FROM EVERY NIÑA SHE FINDS.
THAT'S A HORRIBLE STORY.
THAT'S MALINCHE'S STORY.
I'M SORRY I RUINED YOUR PARTY.
IT'S NO PARTY IF ALL MY GIRLS AREN'T THERE.
COME ON, IT'S TIME FOR FIRE-WORKS. SABES?
YOU'LL PICK IT UP.
NO.

CHAPTER 4

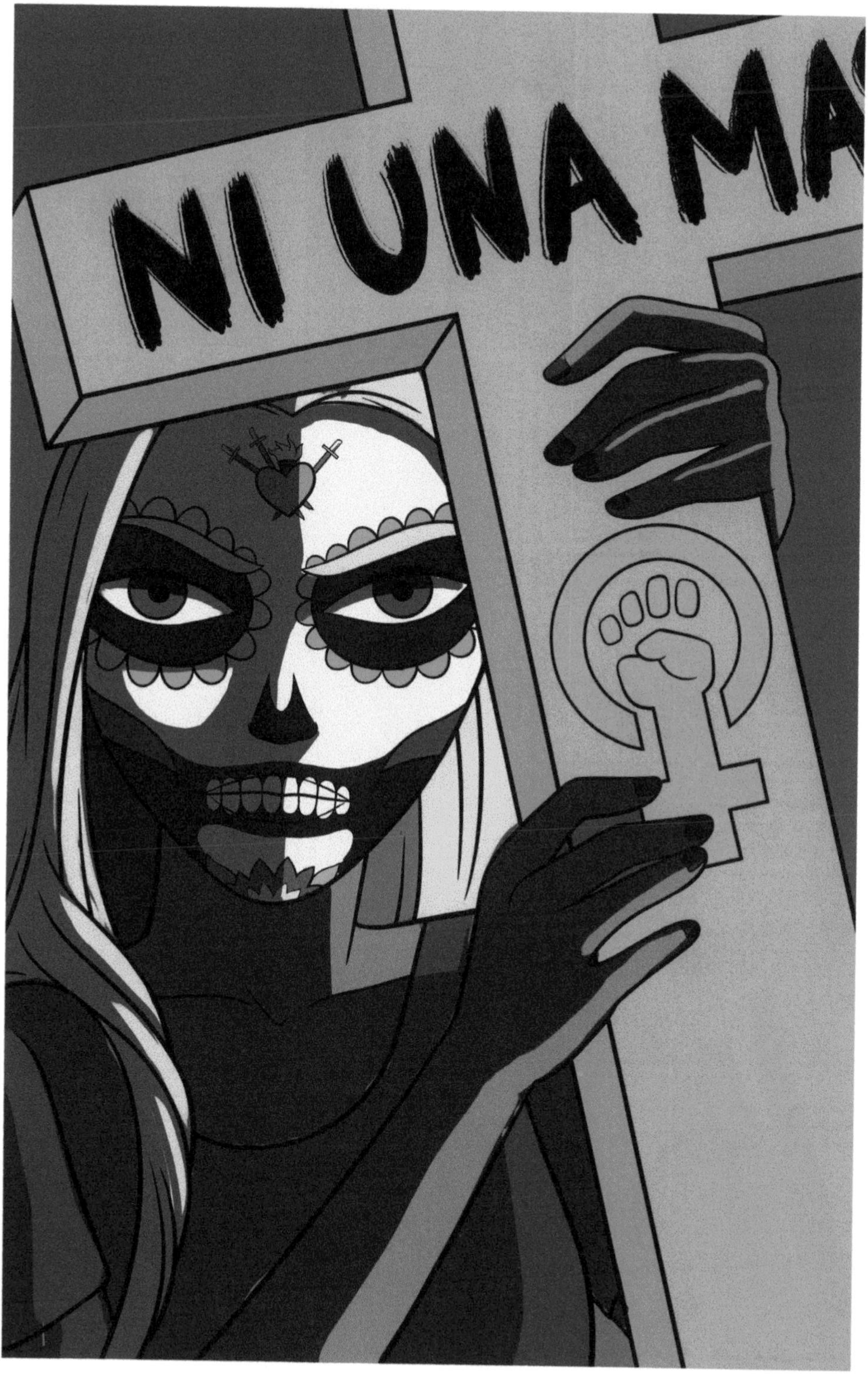
NI UNA MAS

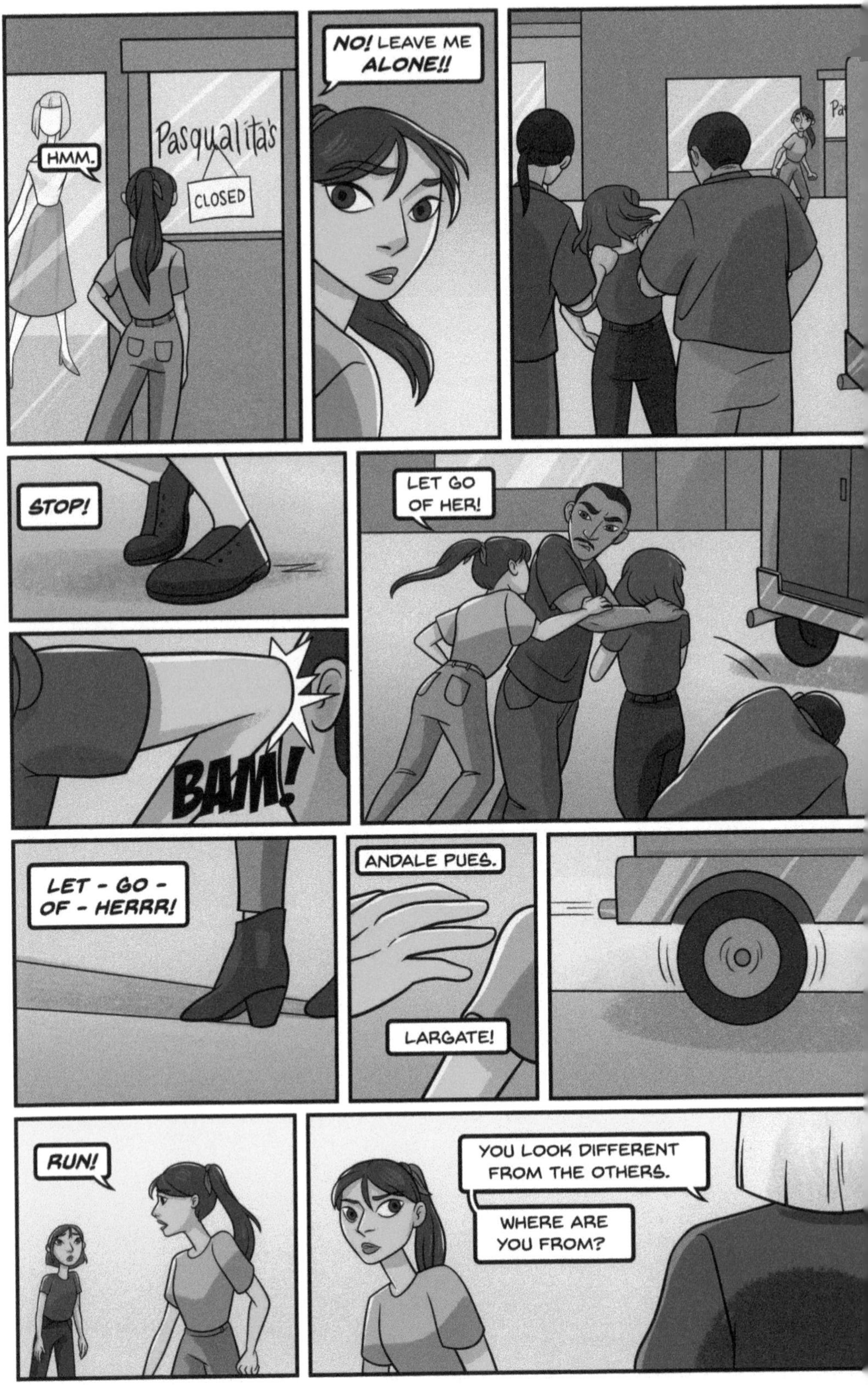
Pasqualita's
CLOSED
HMM.
NO! LEAVE ME ALONE!!
STOP!
BAM!
LET GO OF HER!
LET - GO - OF - HERRR!
ANDALE PUES.
LARGATE!
RUN!
YOU LOOK DIFFERENT FROM THE OTHERS.
WHERE ARE YOU FROM?

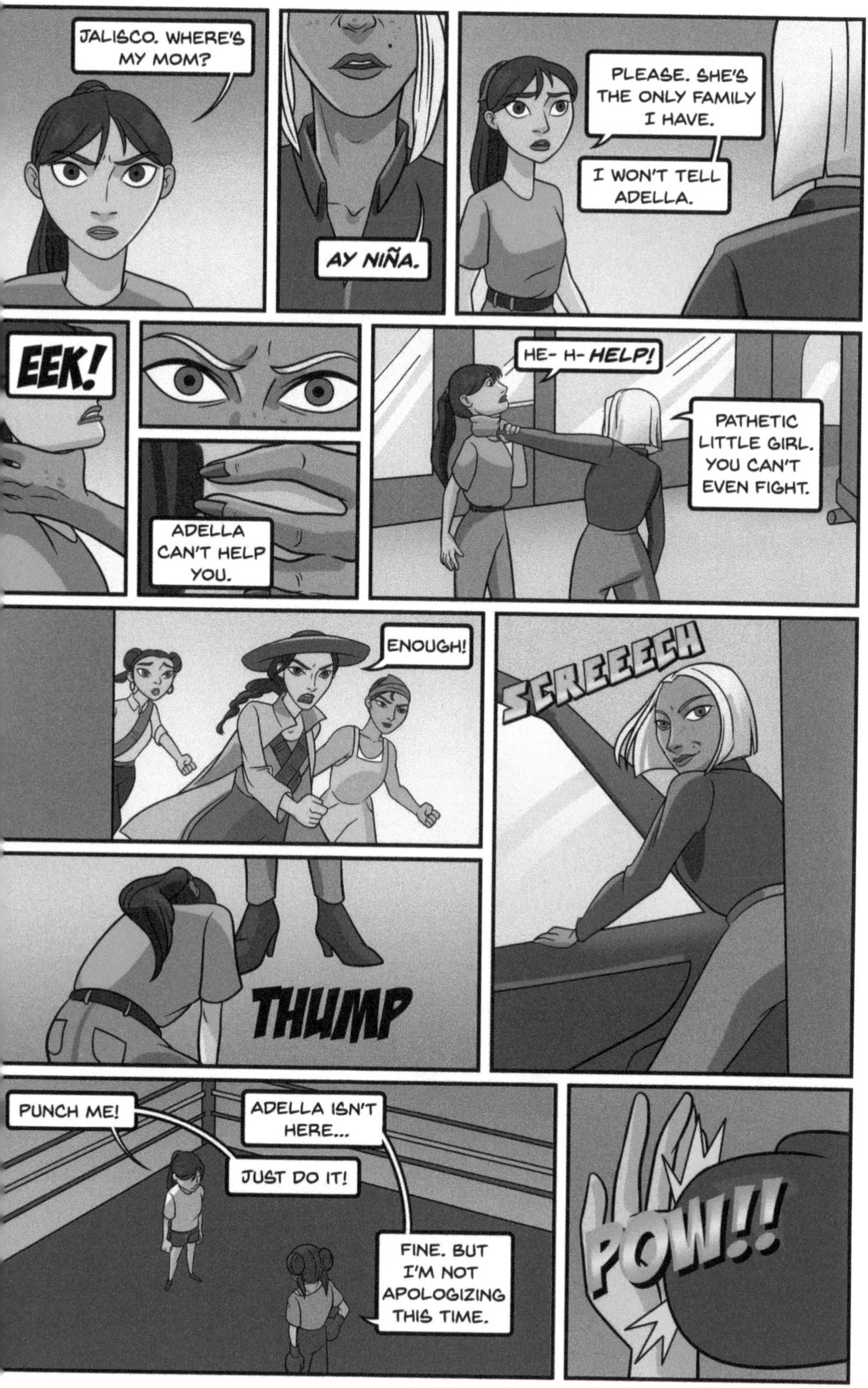
JALISCO. WHERE'S MY MOM?
AY NIÑA.
PLEASE. SHE'S THE ONLY FAMILY I HAVE.
I WON'T TELL ADELLA.
EEK!
ADELLA CAN'T HELP YOU.
HE- H- HELP!
PATHETIC LITTLE GIRL. YOU CAN'T EVEN FIGHT.
ENOUGH!
SCREEECH
THUMP
PUNCH ME!
ADELLA ISN'T HERE...
JUST DO IT!
FINE. BUT I'M NOT APOLOGIZING THIS TIME.
POW!!

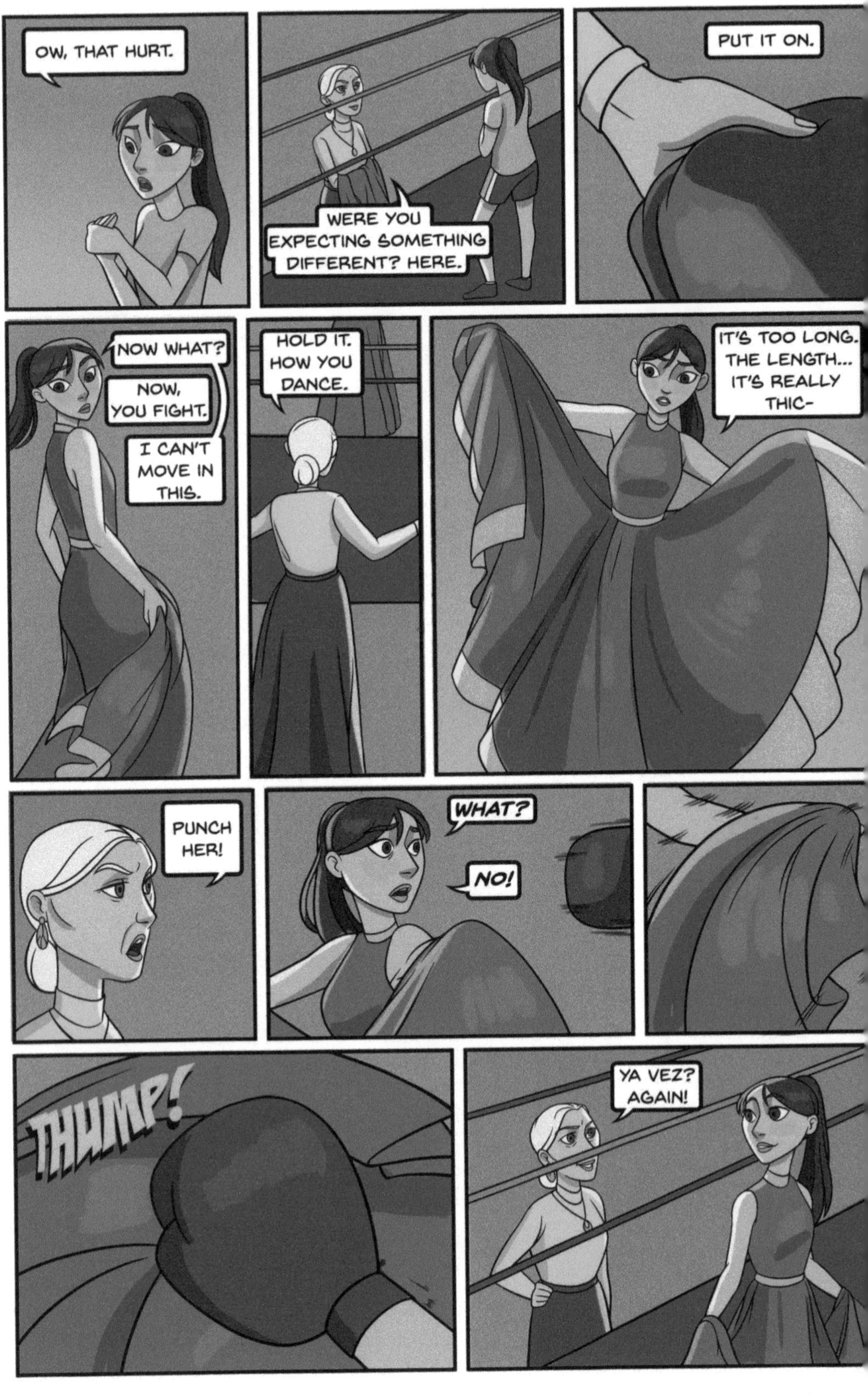
OW, THAT HURT.
WERE YOU EXPECTING SOMETHING DIFFERENT? HERE.
PUT IT ON.
NOW WHAT?
NOW, YOU FIGHT.
I CAN'T MOVE IN THIS.
HOLD IT. HOW YOU DANCE.
IT'S TOO LONG. THE LENGTH... IT'S REALLY THIC-
PUNCH HER!
WHAT?
NO!
THUMP!
YA VEZ? AGAIN!

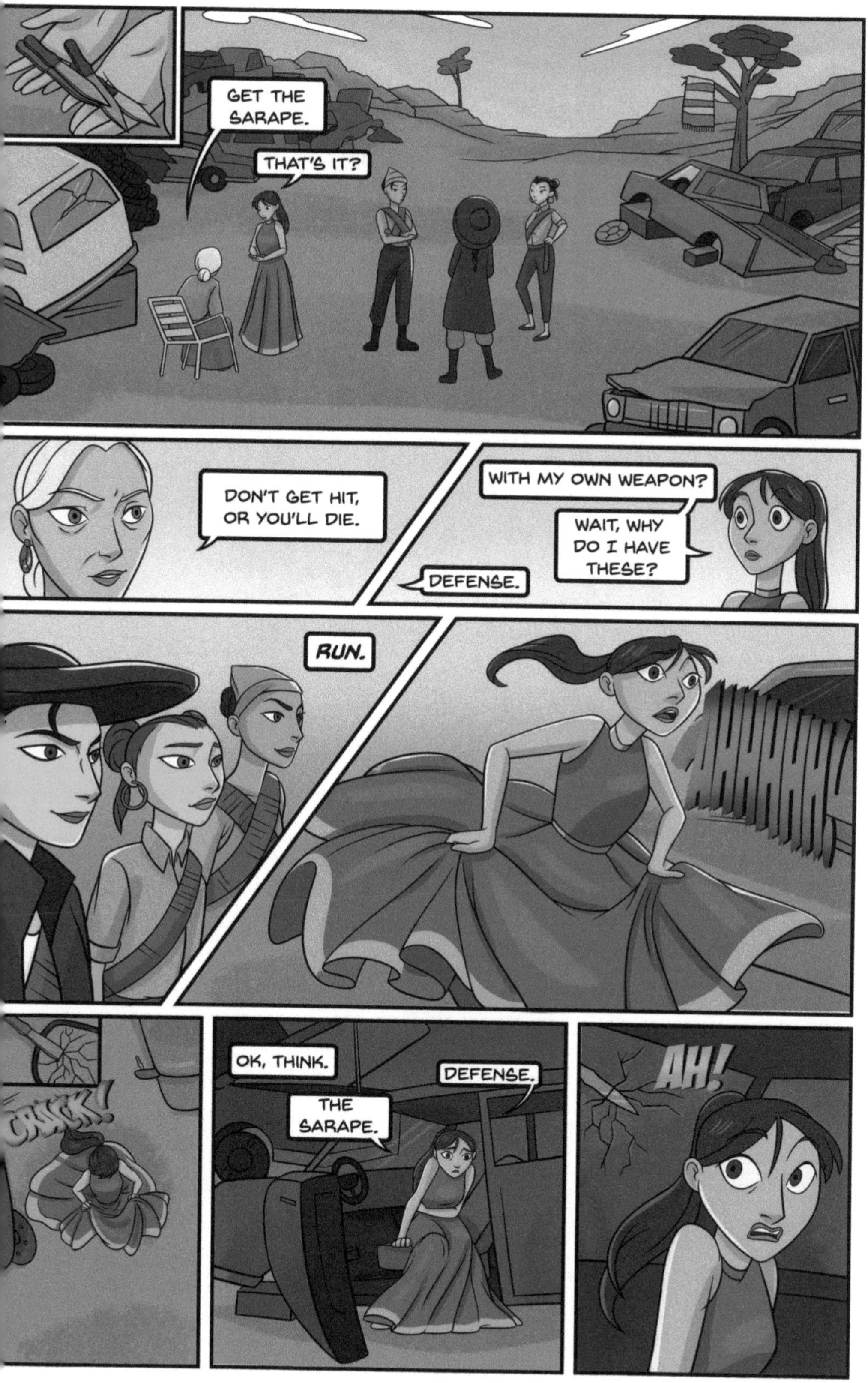

GET THE SARAPE.
THAT'S IT?
DON'T GET HIT, OR YOU'LL DIE.
WITH MY OWN WEAPON?
WAIT, WHY DO I HAVE THESE?
DEFENSE.
RUN.
CRICK!
OK, THINK.
DEFENSE.
THE SARAPE.
AH!

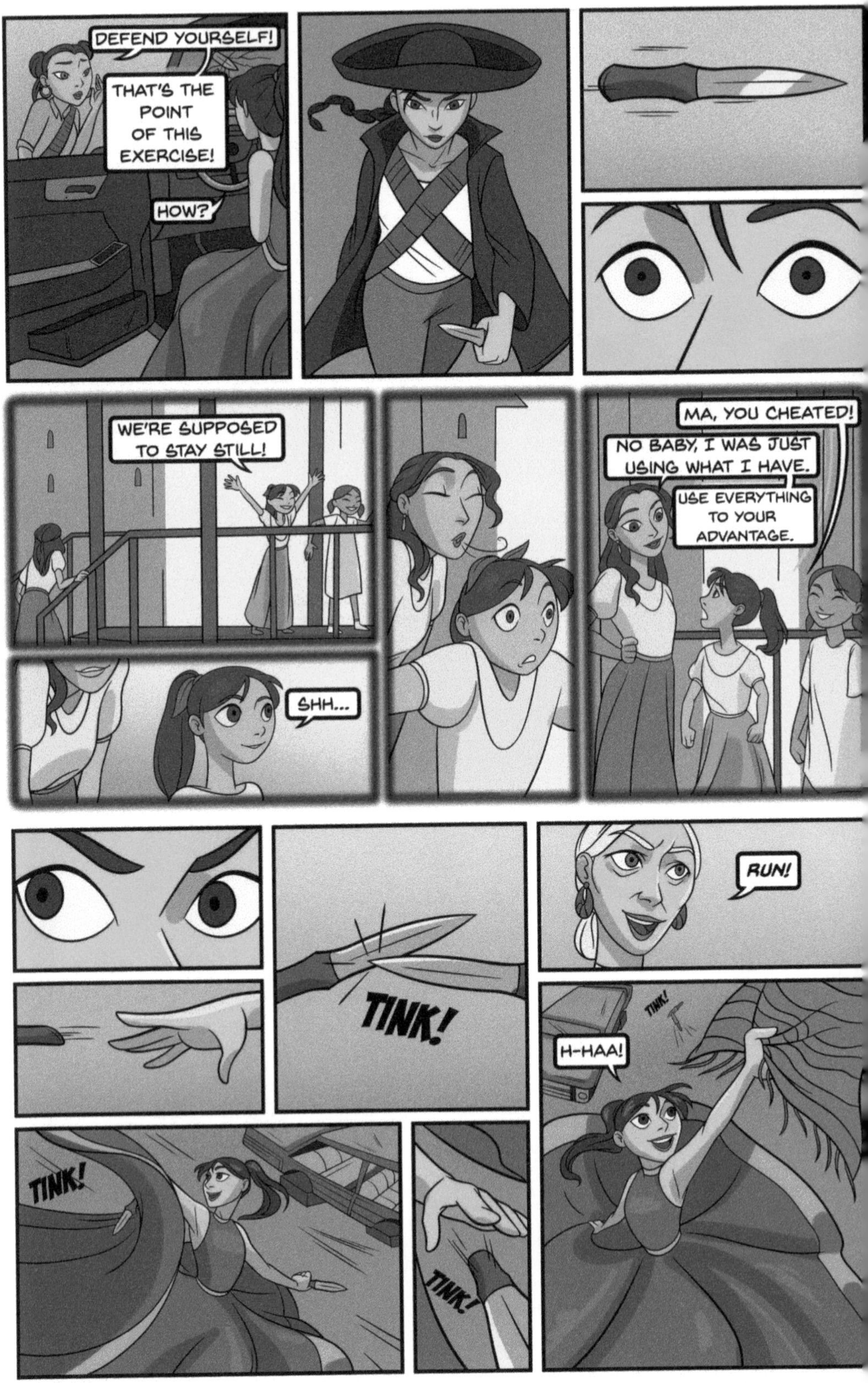
DEFEND YOURSELF!
THAT'S THE POINT OF THIS EXERCISE!
HOW?
WE'RE SUPPOSED TO STAY STILL!
SHH...
MA, YOU CHEATED!
NO BABY, I WAS JUST USING WHAT I HAVE.
USE EVERYTHING TO YOUR ADVANTAGE.
RUN!
TINK!
H-HAA!
TINK!
TINK!
TINK!

CHAPTER 5

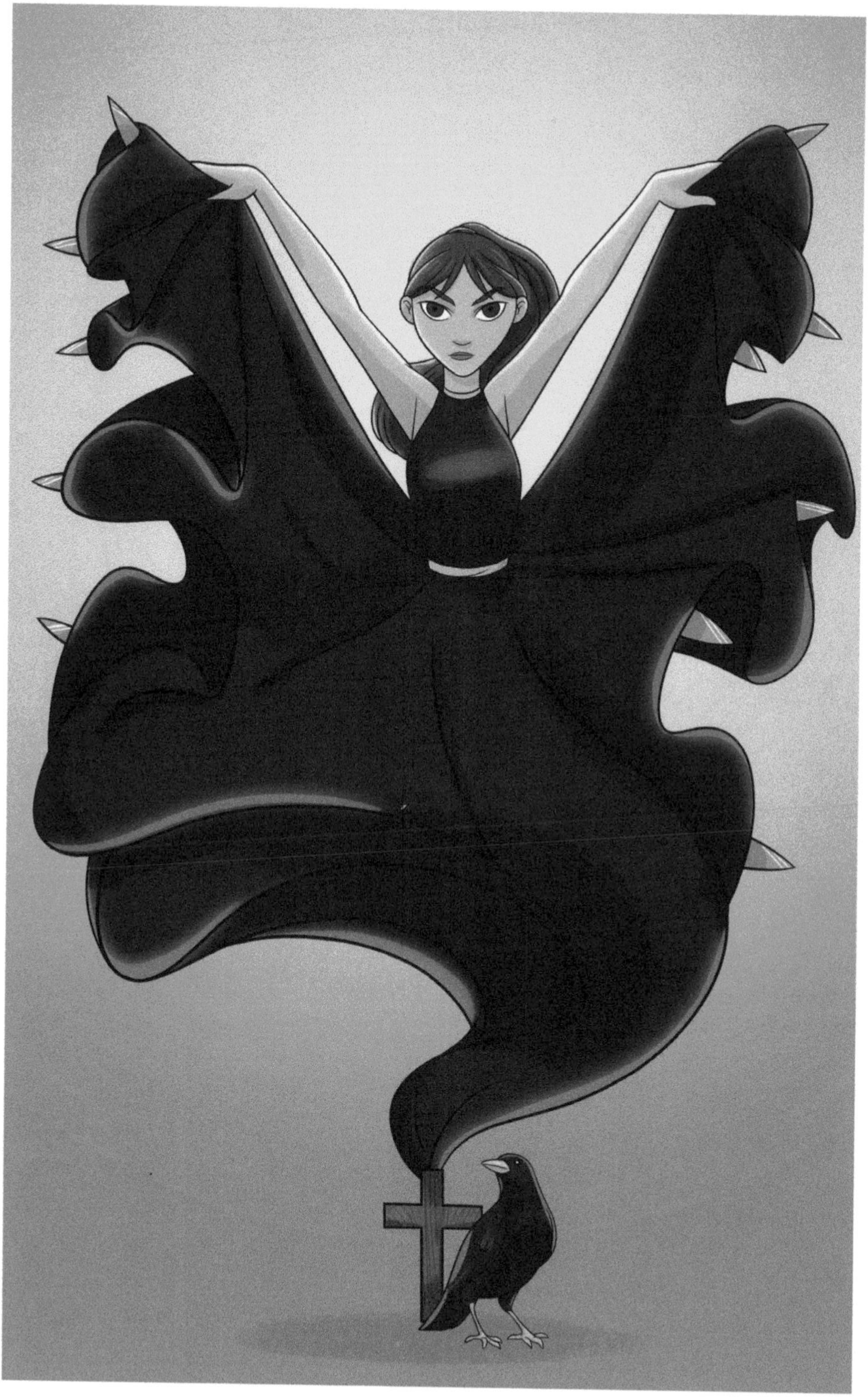

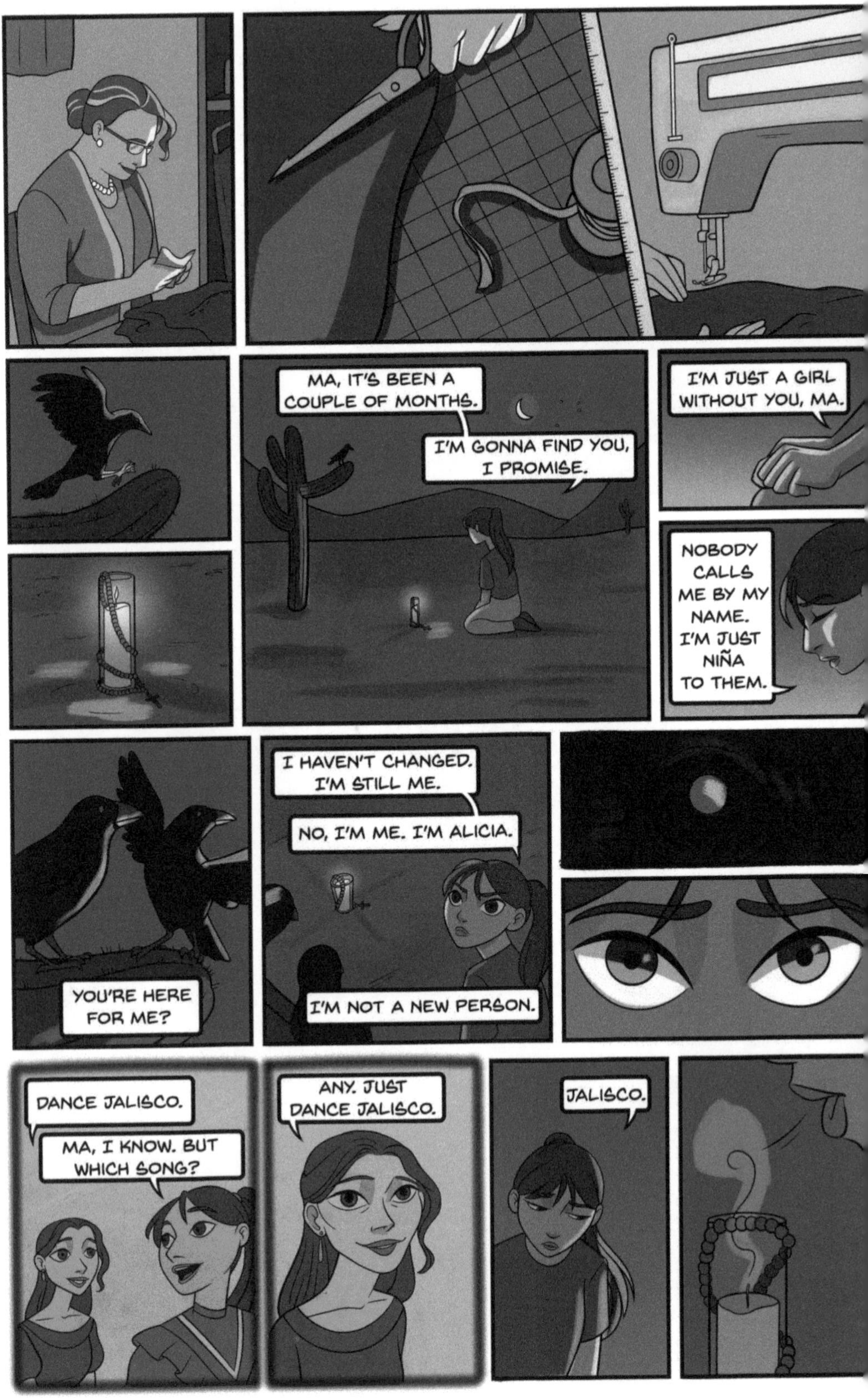
MA, IT'S BEEN A COUPLE OF MONTHS.
I'M GONNA FIND YOU, I PROMISE.
I'M JUST A GIRL WITHOUT YOU, MA.
NOBODY CALLS ME BY MY NAME. I'M JUST NIÑA TO THEM.
YOU'RE HERE FOR ME?
I HAVEN'T CHANGED. I'M STILL ME.
NO, I'M ME. I'M ALICIA.
I'M NOT A NEW PERSON.
DANCE JALISCO.
MA, I KNOW. BUT WHICH SONG?
ANY. JUST DANCE JALISCO.
JALISCO.

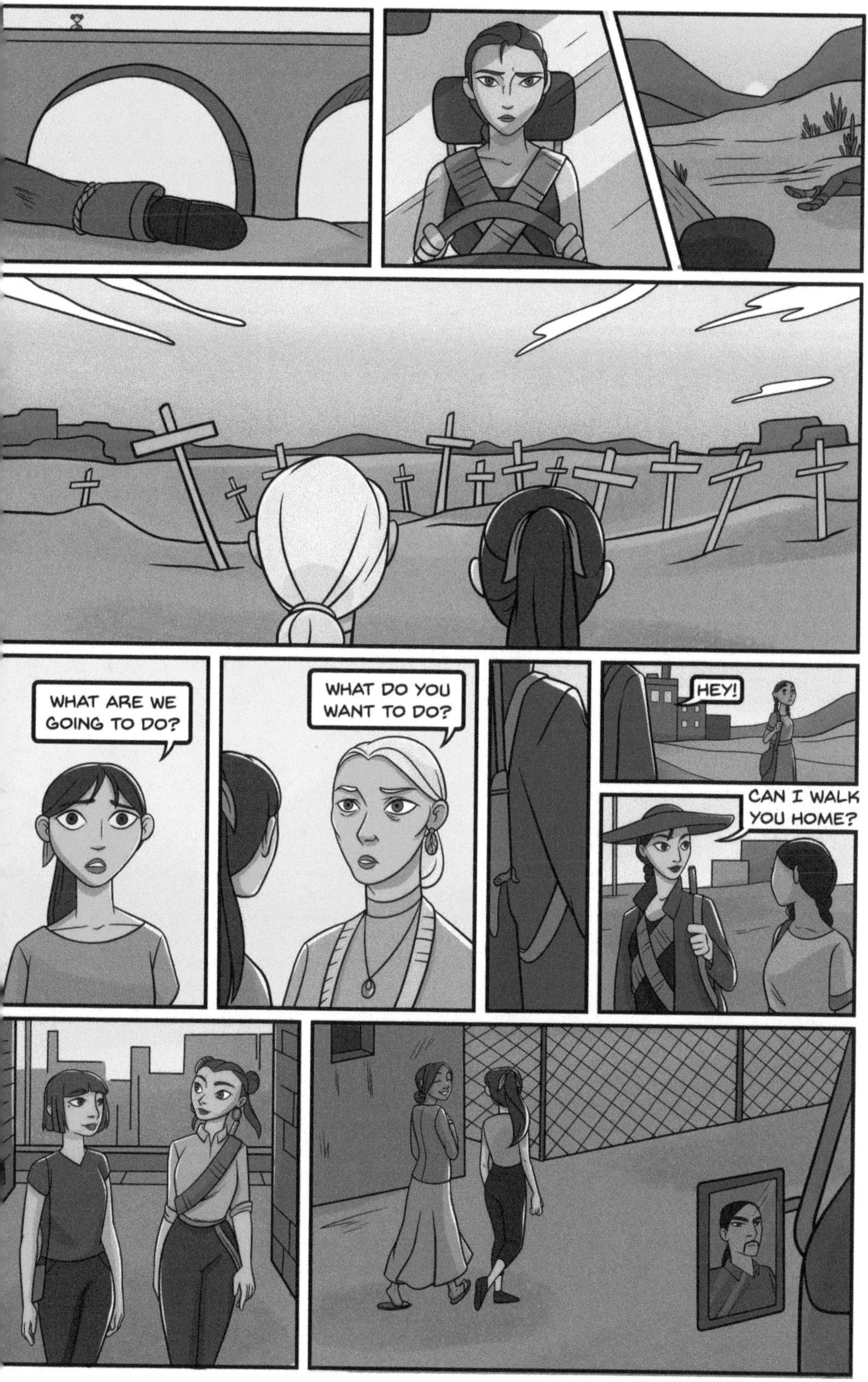
WHAT ARE WE GOING TO DO?
WHAT DO YOU WANT TO DO?
HEY!
CAN I WALK YOU HOME?

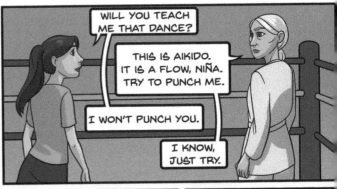

WILL YOU TEACH ME THAT DANCE?

THIS IS AIKIDO. IT IS A FLOW, NIÑA. TRY TO PUNCH ME.

I WON'T PUNCH YOU.

I KNOW, JUST TRY.

WHOOSH!

SLAM!

I WASN'T EXPECTING THIS.

PRECISELY. NOW YOU TRY.

YOU **NEVER** TAUGHT ME THIS! **I** SHOULD KNOW THIS, AS YOUR DAUGHTER. NOT THIS...THIS...

CALMATE!

WILL YOU LEAVE US FOR A MOMENT?

SURE.

WOULD YOU SAVE YOUR SISTER IF GIVEN THE CHANCE?

I DON'T HAVE A SISTER.

SAY YOU DID, AND YOUR MOM TREATED HER DIFFERENTLY BECAUSE OF HER SKIN TONE, WOULD YOU DEFEND HER?

UM, YEAH, I GUESS.

AGAINST YOUR OWN MOTHER?

AGAINST ANYONE.

WHY?

BECAUSE... SHE'S MY SISTER, A HUMAN BEING. AND COLOR DOESN'T MATTER.

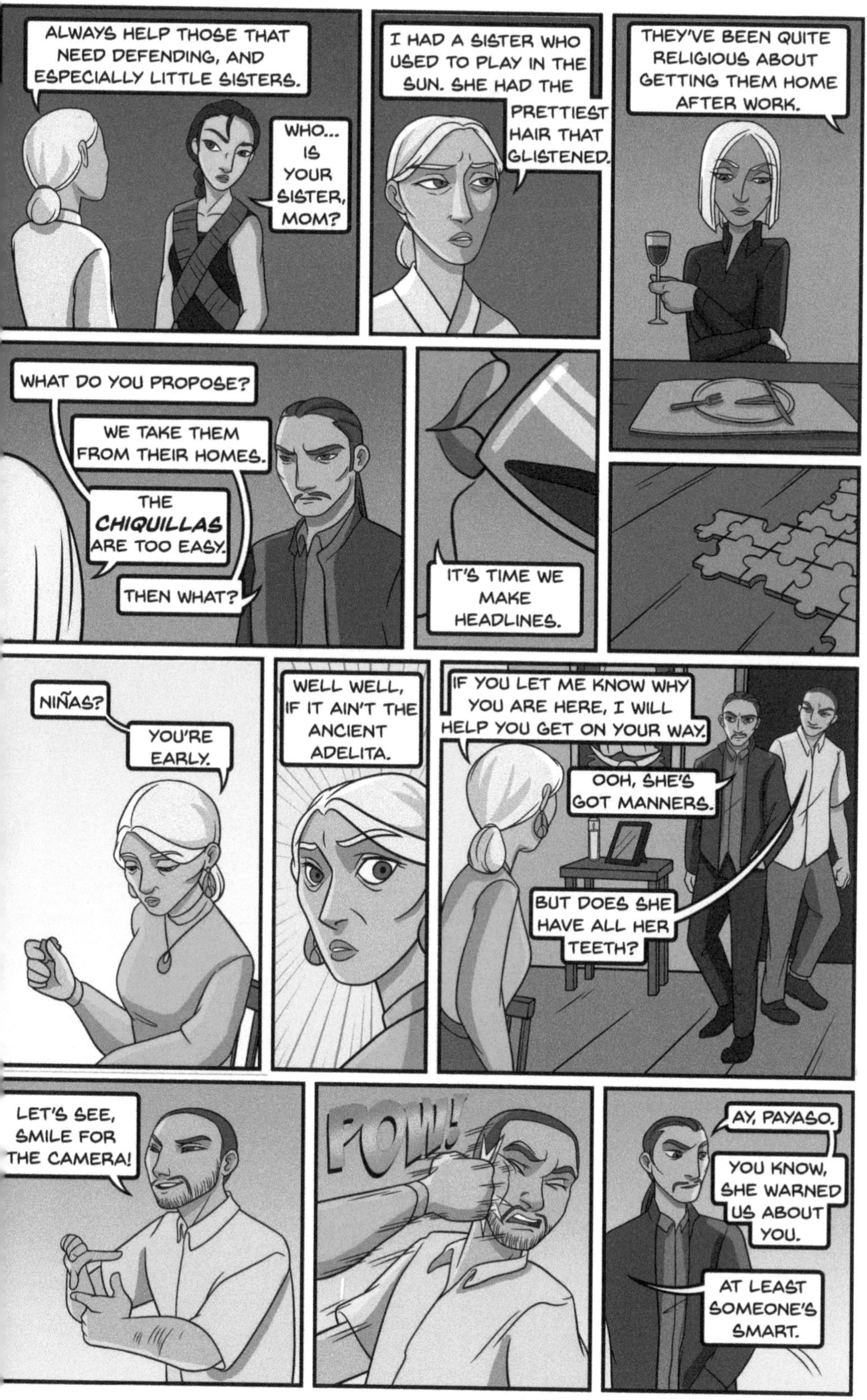
ALWAYS HELP THOSE THAT NEED DEFENDING, AND ESPECIALLY LITTLE SISTERS.
WHO... IS YOUR SISTER, MOM?
I HAD A SISTER WHO USED TO PLAY IN THE SUN. SHE HAD THE
PRETTIEST HAIR THAT GLISTENED.
THEY'VE BEEN QUITE RELIGIOUS ABOUT GETTING THEM HOME AFTER WORK.
WHAT DO YOU PROPOSE?
WE TAKE THEM FROM THEIR HOMES.
THE *CHIQUILLAS* ARE TOO EASY.
THEN WHAT?
IT'S TIME WE MAKE HEADLINES.
NIÑAS?
YOU'RE EARLY.
WELL WELL, IF IT AIN'T THE ANCIENT ADELITA.
IF YOU LET ME KNOW WHY YOU ARE HERE, I WILL HELP YOU GET ON YOUR WAY.
OOH, SHE'S GOT MANNERS.
BUT DOES SHE HAVE ALL HER TEETH?
LET'S SEE, SMILE FOR THE CAMERA!
POW!
AY, PAYASO.
YOU KNOW, SHE WARNED US ABOUT YOU.
AT LEAST SOMEONE'S SMART.

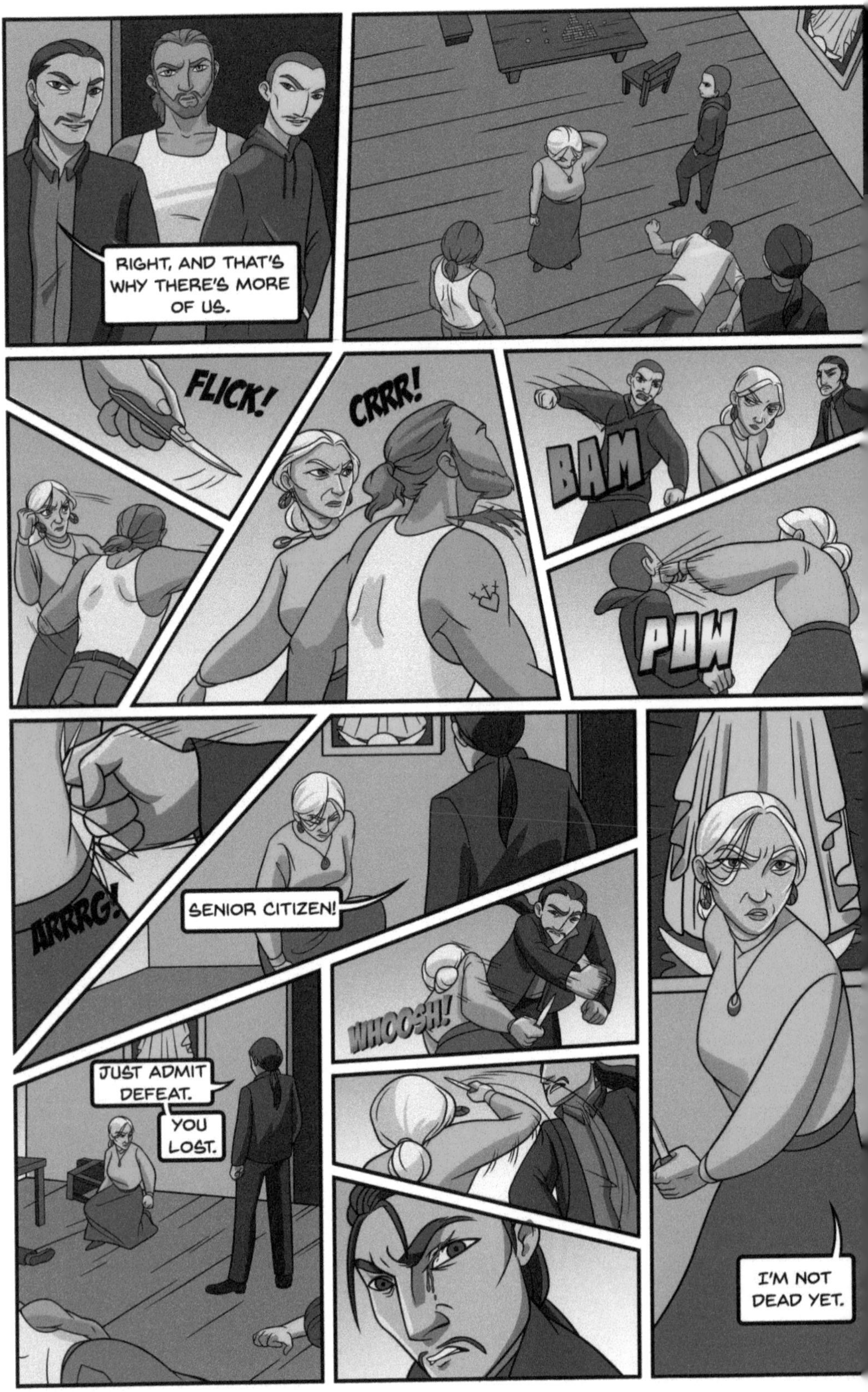
RIGHT, AND THAT'S WHY THERE'S MORE OF US.
FLICK!
CRRR!
BAM
POW
ARRRG!
SENIOR CITIZEN!
WHOOSH!
JUST ADMIT DEFEAT.
YOU LOST.
I'M NOT DEAD YET.

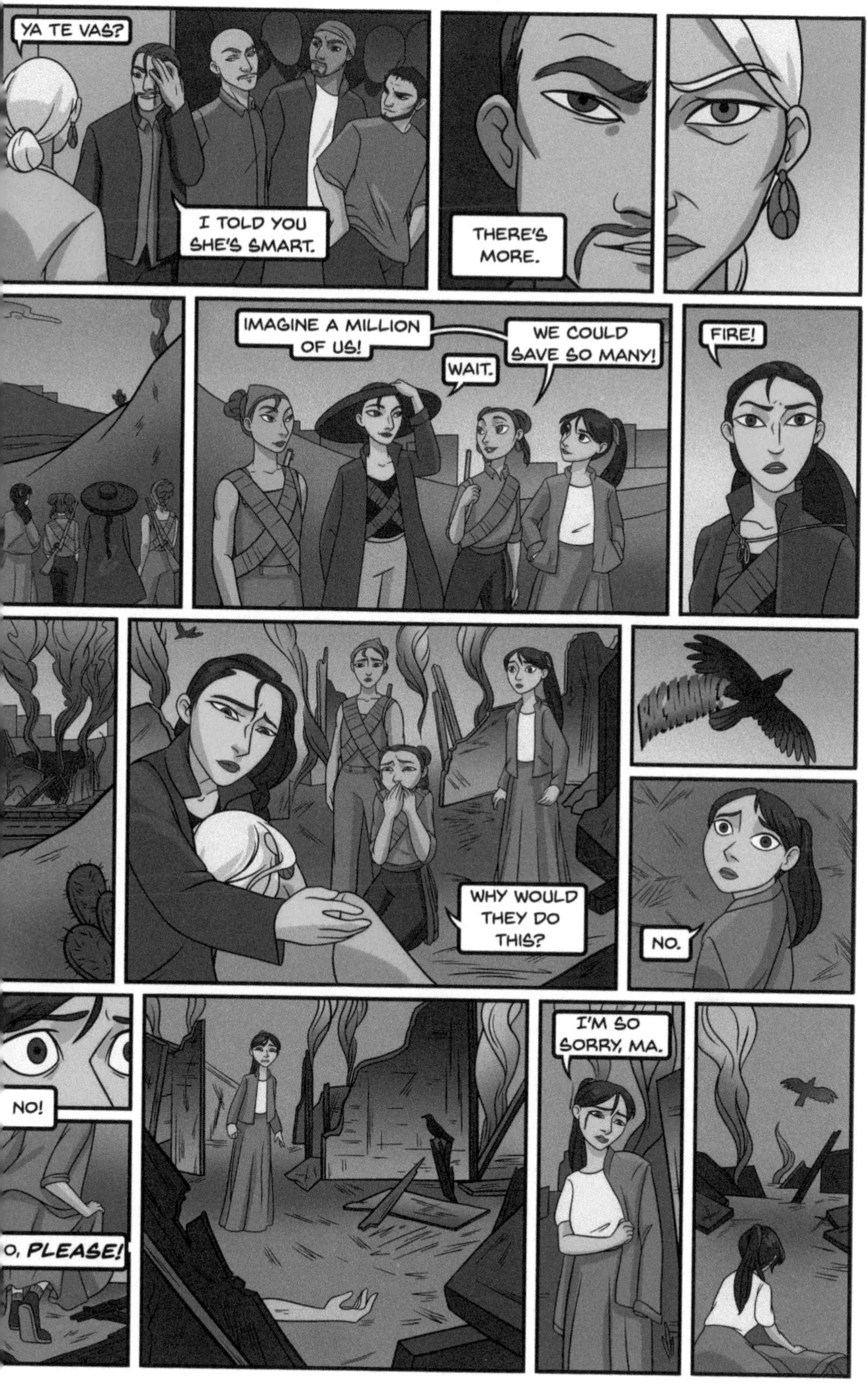
YA TE VAS?
I TOLD YOU SHE'S SMART.
THERE'S MORE.
IMAGINE A MILLION OF US!
WE COULD SAVE SO MANY!
WAIT.
FIRE!
WHY WOULD THEY DO THIS?
NO.
NO!
O, PLEASE!
I'M SO SORRY, MA.

CHAPTER 6

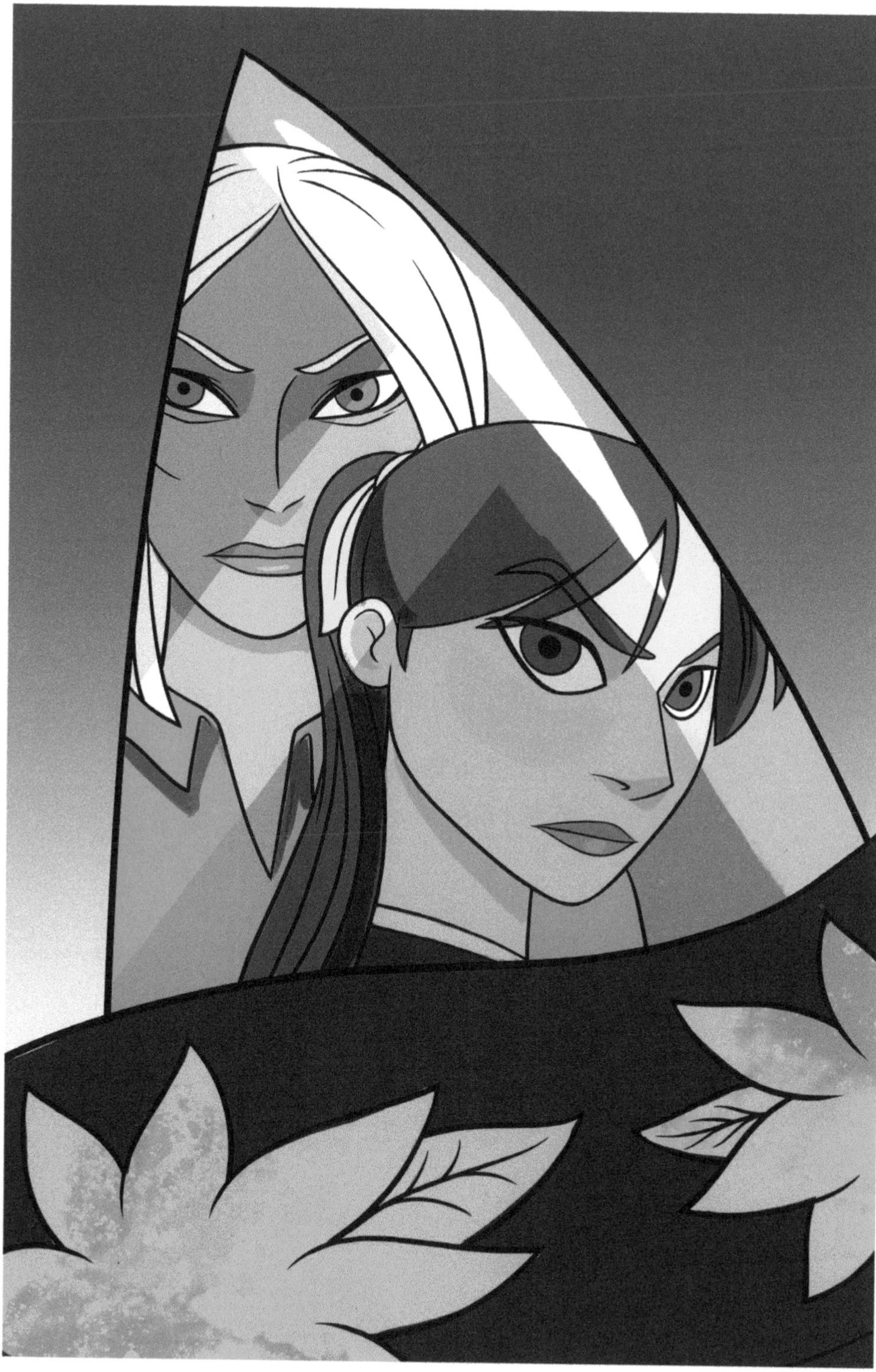

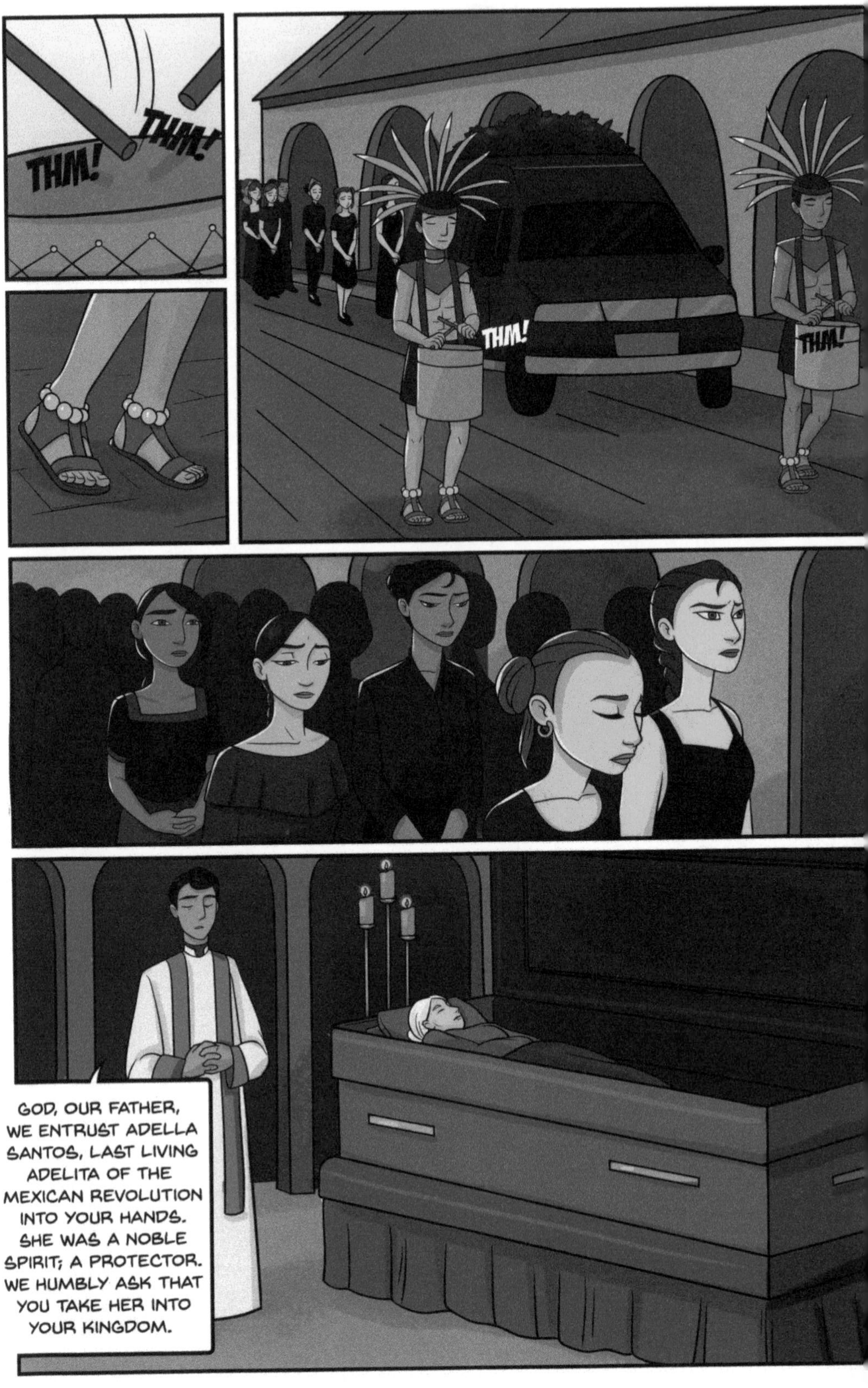
THM!
THM!
THM!
THM!
GOD, OUR FATHER, WE ENTRUST ADELLA SANTOS, LAST LIVING ADELITA OF THE MEXICAN REVOLUTION INTO YOUR HANDS. SHE WAS A NOBLE SPIRIT; A PROTECTOR. WE HUMBLY ASK THAT YOU TAKE HER INTO YOUR KINGDOM.

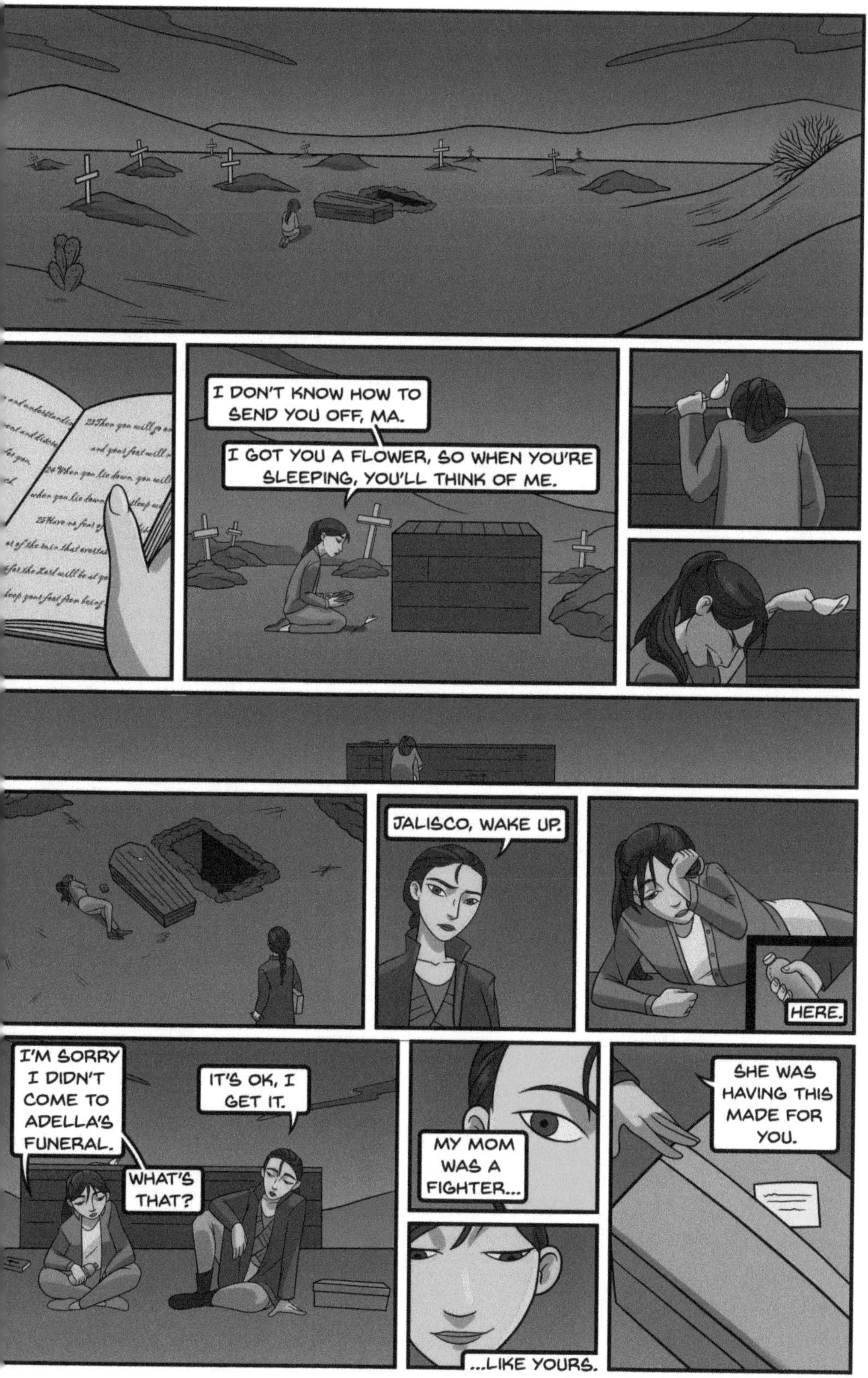
I DON'T KNOW HOW TO SEND YOU OFF, MA.
I GOT YOU A FLOWER, SO WHEN YOU'RE SLEEPING, YOU'LL THINK OF ME.
JALISCO, WAKE UP.
HERE.
I'M SORRY I DIDN'T COME TO ADELLA'S FUNERAL.
IT'S OK, I GET IT.
WHAT'S THAT?
MY MOM WAS A FIGHTER...
...LIKE YOURS.
SHE WAS HAVING THIS MADE FOR YOU.

JALISCO

never waste your pain

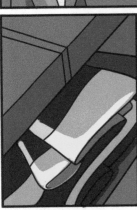

AY!

HMMM.

I'M GONNA MAKE THINGS RIGHT.

I PROMISE.

HEY, WAIT UP!

SOOO...

YOU WANT ME TO GO WITH YOU TWO...

A GIRL WHO JUST LEARNED TO FIGHT.

AND YOU, A TRAINER.

TO KILL MALINCHE?

YES.

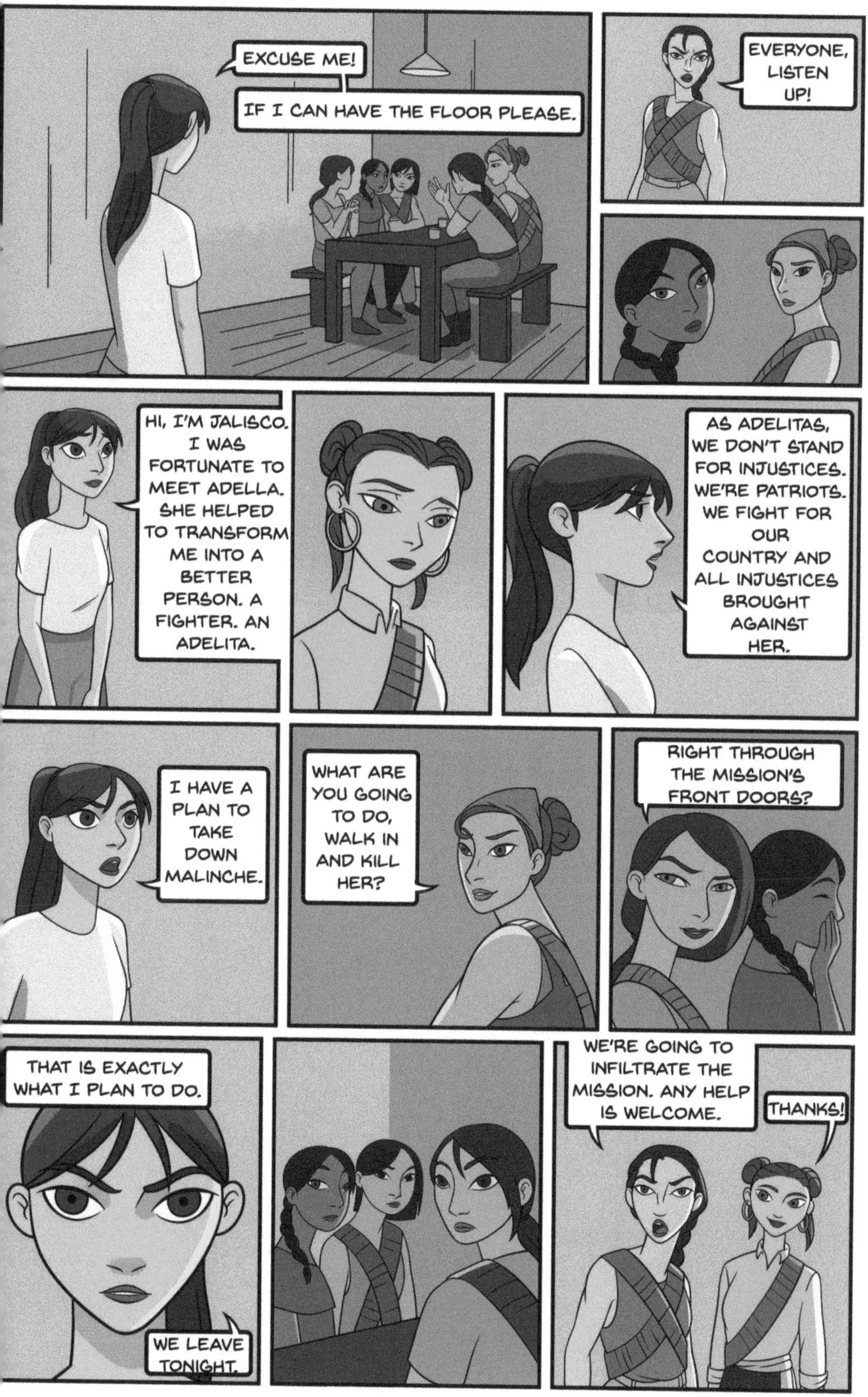
EXCUSE ME!
IF I CAN HAVE THE FLOOR PLEASE.
EVERYONE, LISTEN UP!
HI, I'M JALISCO. I WAS FORTUNATE TO MEET ADELLA. SHE HELPED TO TRANSFORM ME INTO A BETTER PERSON. A FIGHTER. AN ADELITA.
AS ADELITAS, WE DON'T STAND FOR INJUSTICES. WE'RE PATRIOTS. WE FIGHT FOR OUR COUNTRY AND ALL INJUSTICES BROUGHT AGAINST HER.
I HAVE A PLAN TO TAKE DOWN MALINCHE.
WHAT ARE YOU GOING TO DO, WALK IN AND KILL HER?
RIGHT THROUGH THE MISSION'S FRONT DOORS?
THAT IS EXACTLY WHAT I PLAN TO DO.
WE LEAVE TONIGHT.
WE'RE GOING TO INFILTRATE THE MISSION. ANY HELP IS WELCOME.
THANKS!

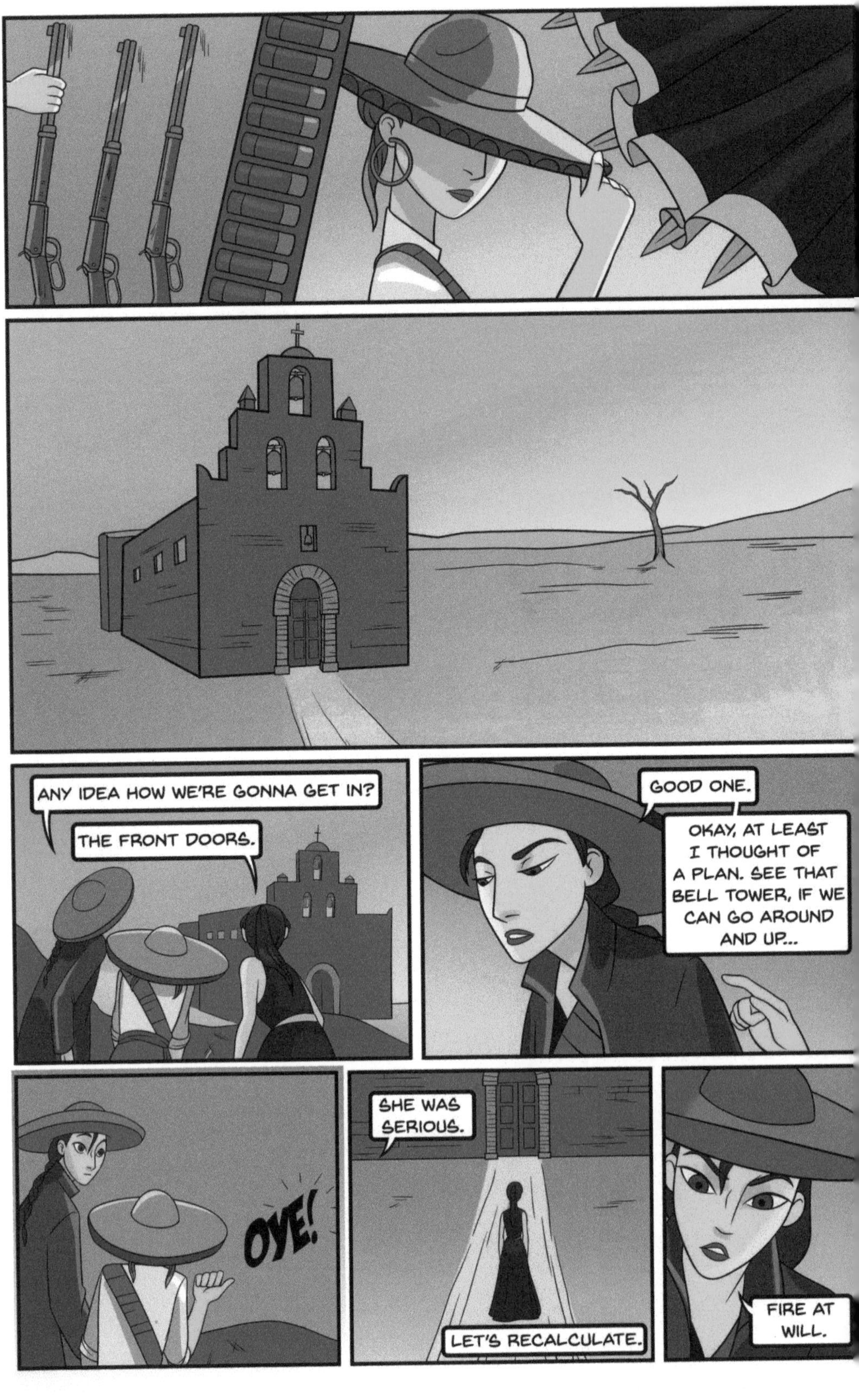
ANY IDEA HOW WE'RE GONNA GET IN?
THE FRONT DOORS.
GOOD ONE.
OKAY, AT LEAST I THOUGHT OF A PLAN. SEE THAT BELL TOWER, IF WE CAN GO AROUND AND UP...
OYE!
SHE WAS SERIOUS.
LET'S RECALCULATE.
FIRE AT WILL.

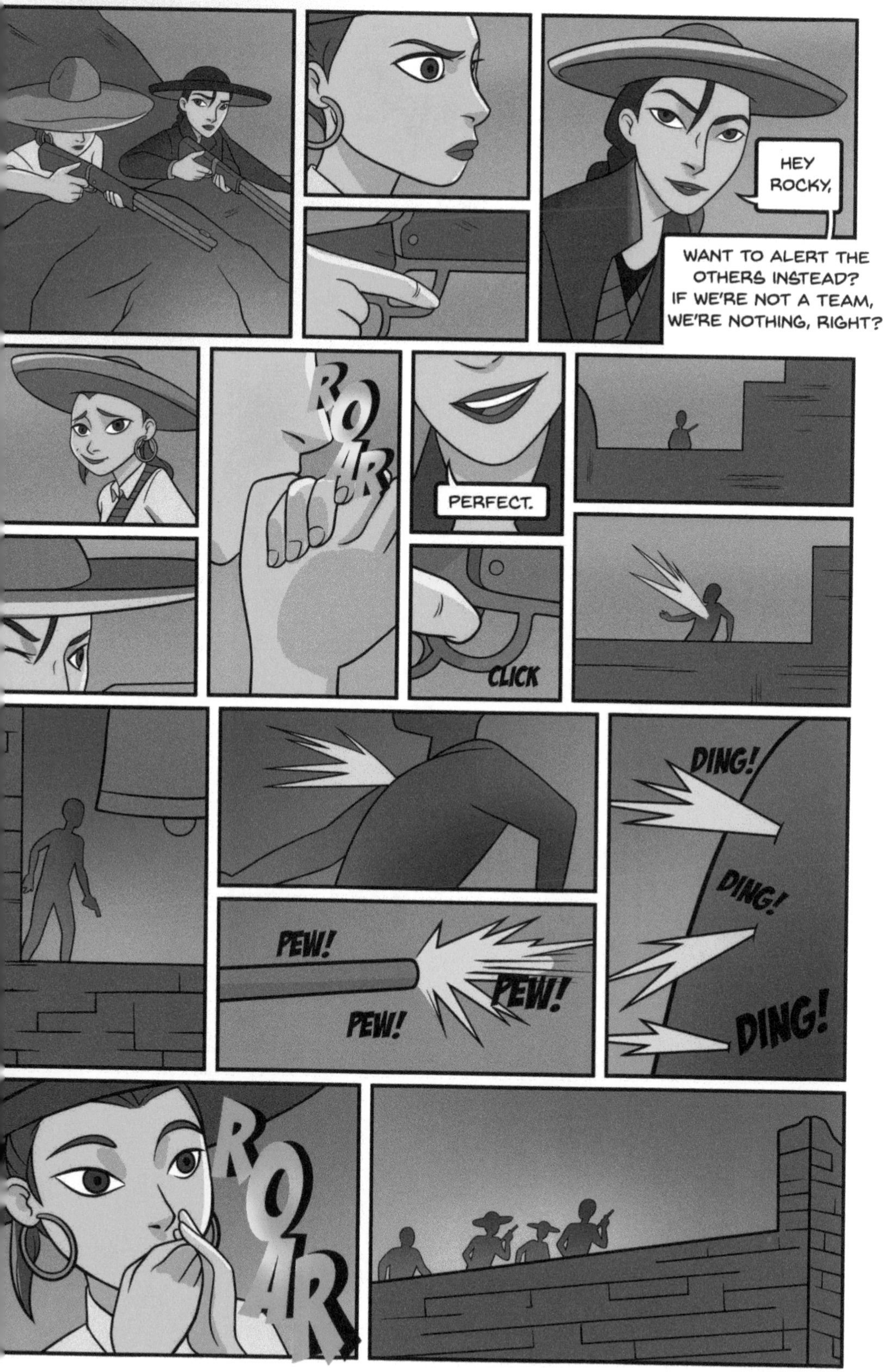
HEY ROCKY,
WANT TO ALERT THE OTHERS INSTEAD? IF WE'RE NOT A TEAM, WE'RE NOTHING, RIGHT?
ROAR
PERFECT.
CLICK
DING!
DING!
PEW!
PEW!
PEW!
DING!
ROAR

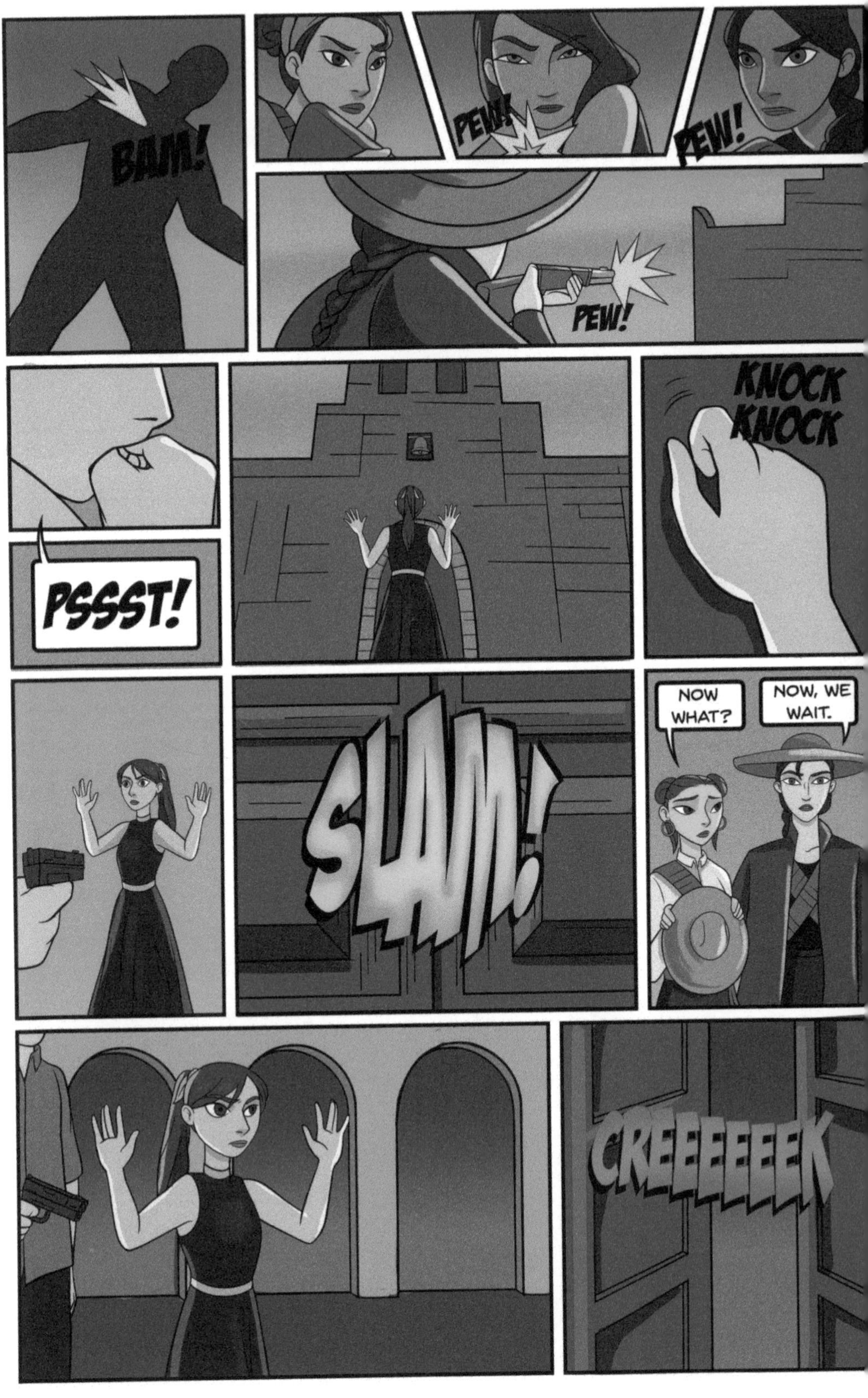
BAM!
PEW!
PEW!
PEW!
KNOCK KNOCK
PSSST!
SLAM!
NOW WHAT?
NOW, WE WAIT.
CREEEEEEK

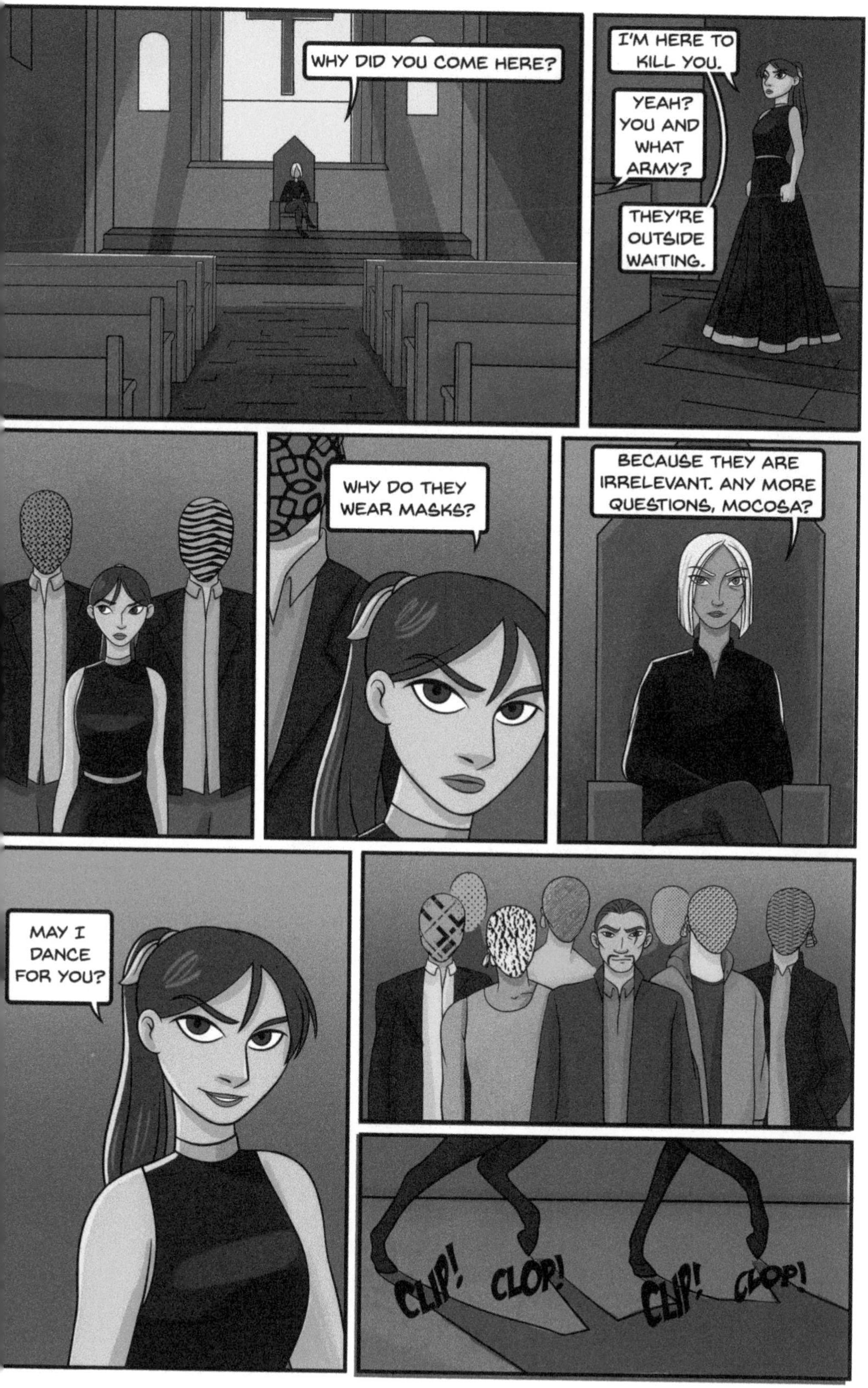
WHY DID YOU COME HERE?
I'M HERE TO KILL YOU.
YEAH? YOU AND WHAT ARMY?
THEY'RE OUTSIDE WAITING.
WHY DO THEY WEAR MASKS?
BECAUSE THEY ARE IRRELEVANT. ANY MORE QUESTIONS, MOCOSA?
MAY I DANCE FOR YOU?
CLIP! CLOP! CLIP! CLOP!

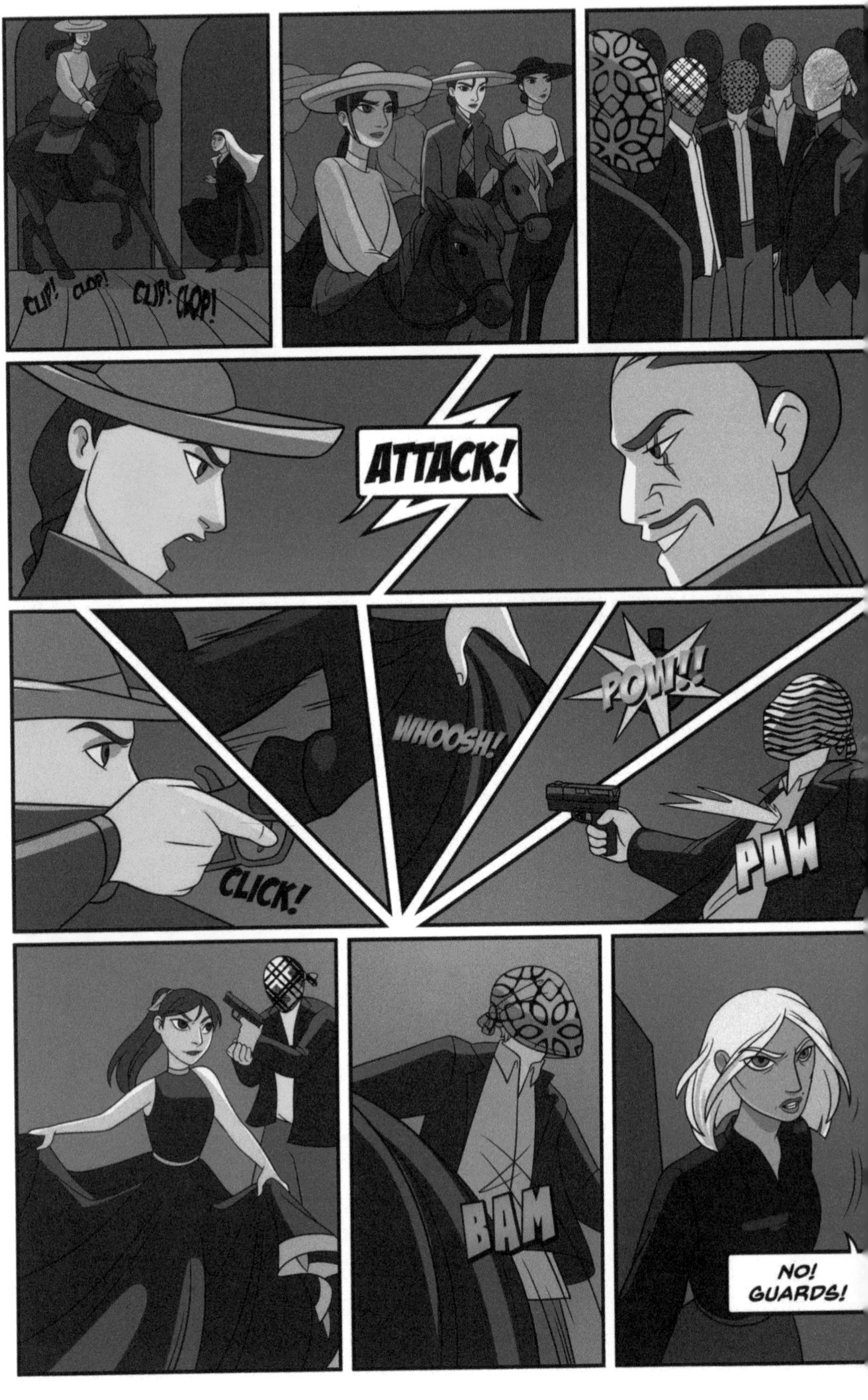
CLIP! CLOP! CLIP! CLOP!
ATTACK!
CLICK!
WHOOSH!
POW!!
POW
BAM
NO! GUARDS!

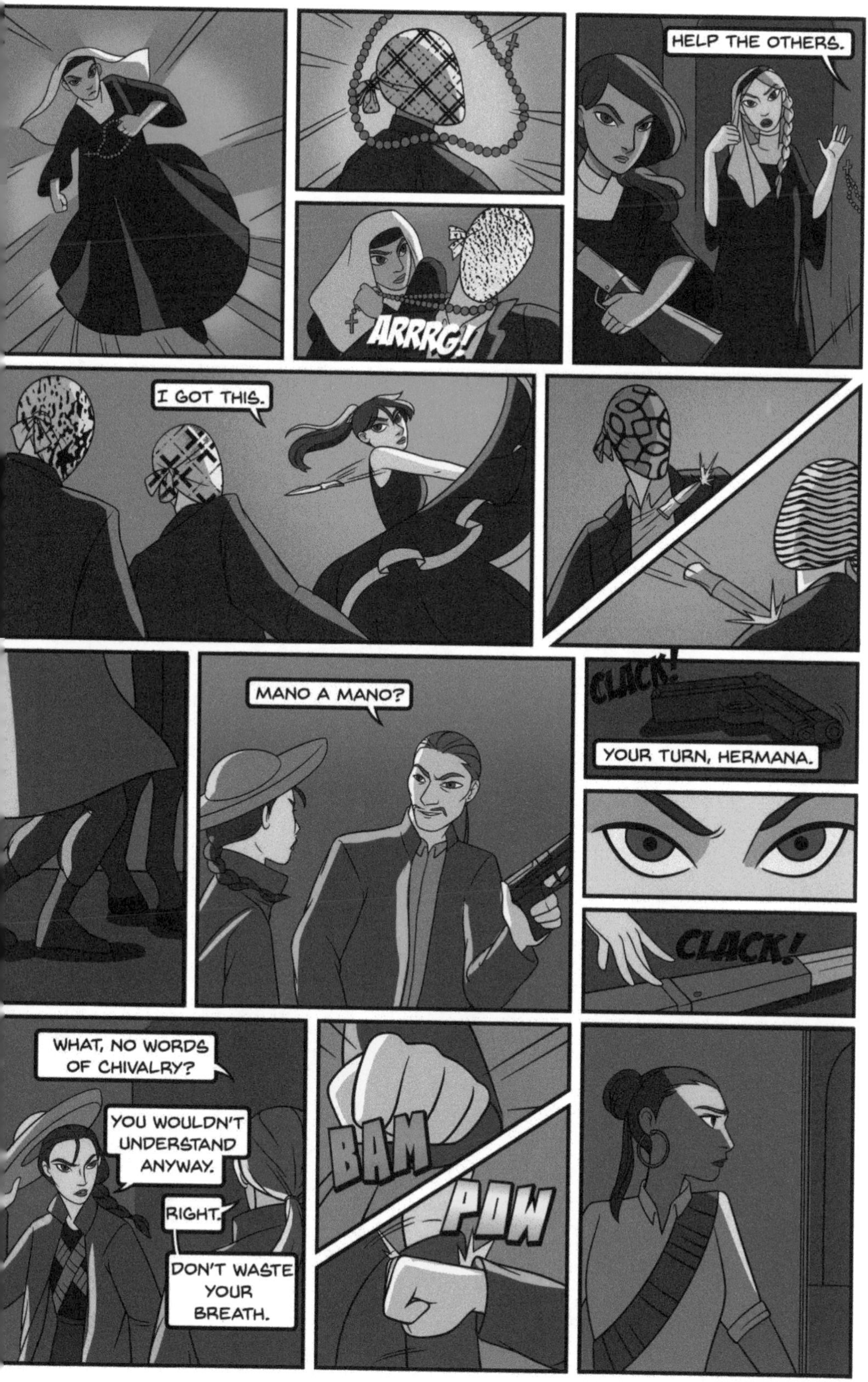
HELP THE OTHERS.
ARRRG!
I GOT THIS.
MANO A MANO?
CLACK!
YOUR TURN, HERMANA.
CLACK!
WHAT, NO WORDS OF CHIVALRY?
YOU WOULDN'T UNDERSTAND ANYWAY.
RIGHT.
DON'T WASTE YOUR BREATH.
BAM
POW

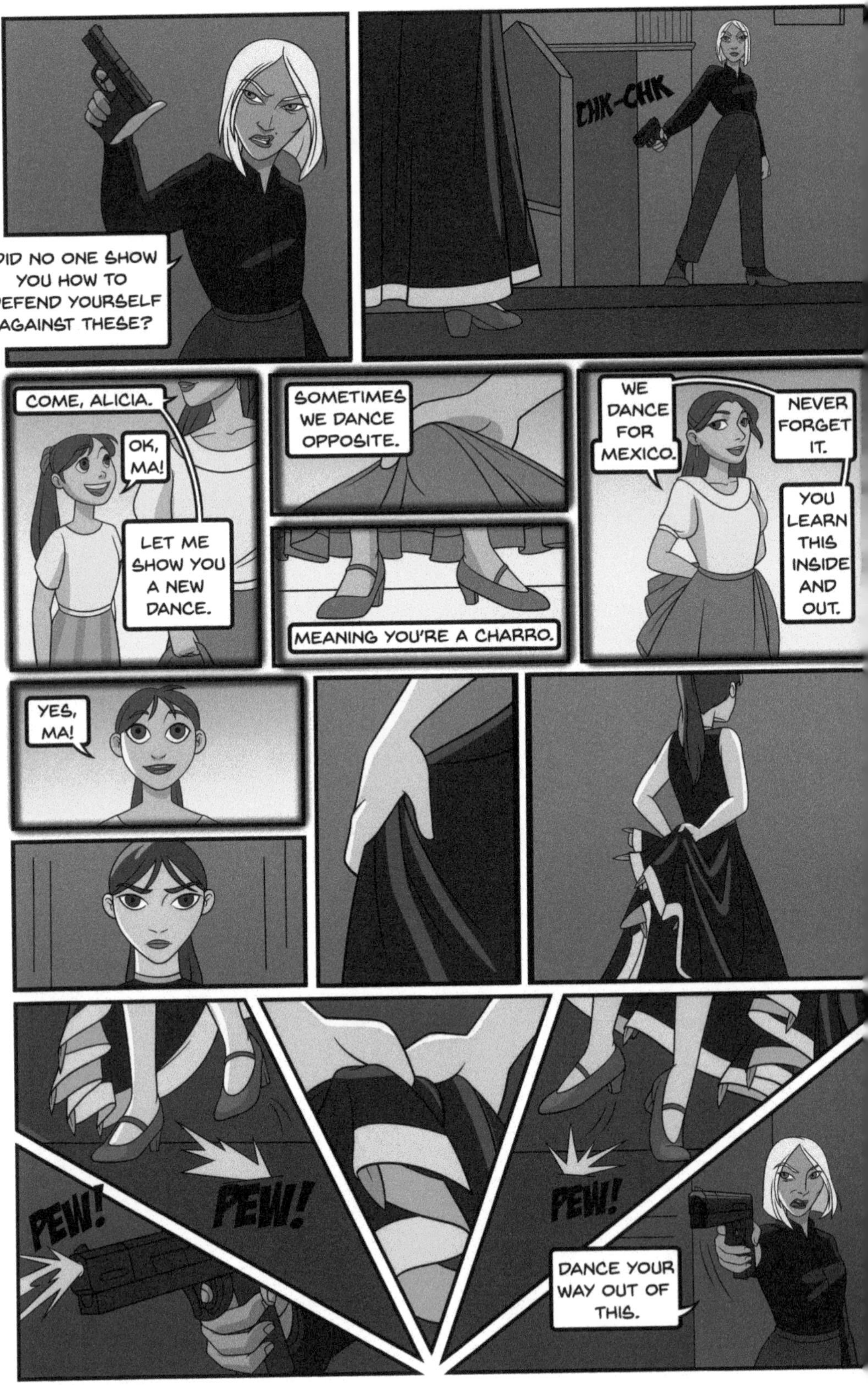
DID NO ONE SHOW YOU HOW TO DEFEND YOURSELF AGAINST THESE?
CHK-CHK
COME, ALICIA.
OK, MA!
LET ME SHOW YOU A NEW DANCE.
SOMETIMES WE DANCE OPPOSITE.
MEANING YOU'RE A CHARRO.
WE DANCE FOR MEXICO.
NEVER FORGET IT.
YOU LEARN THIS INSIDE AND OUT.
YES, MA!
PEW!
PEW!
PEW!
DANCE YOUR WAY OUT OF THIS.

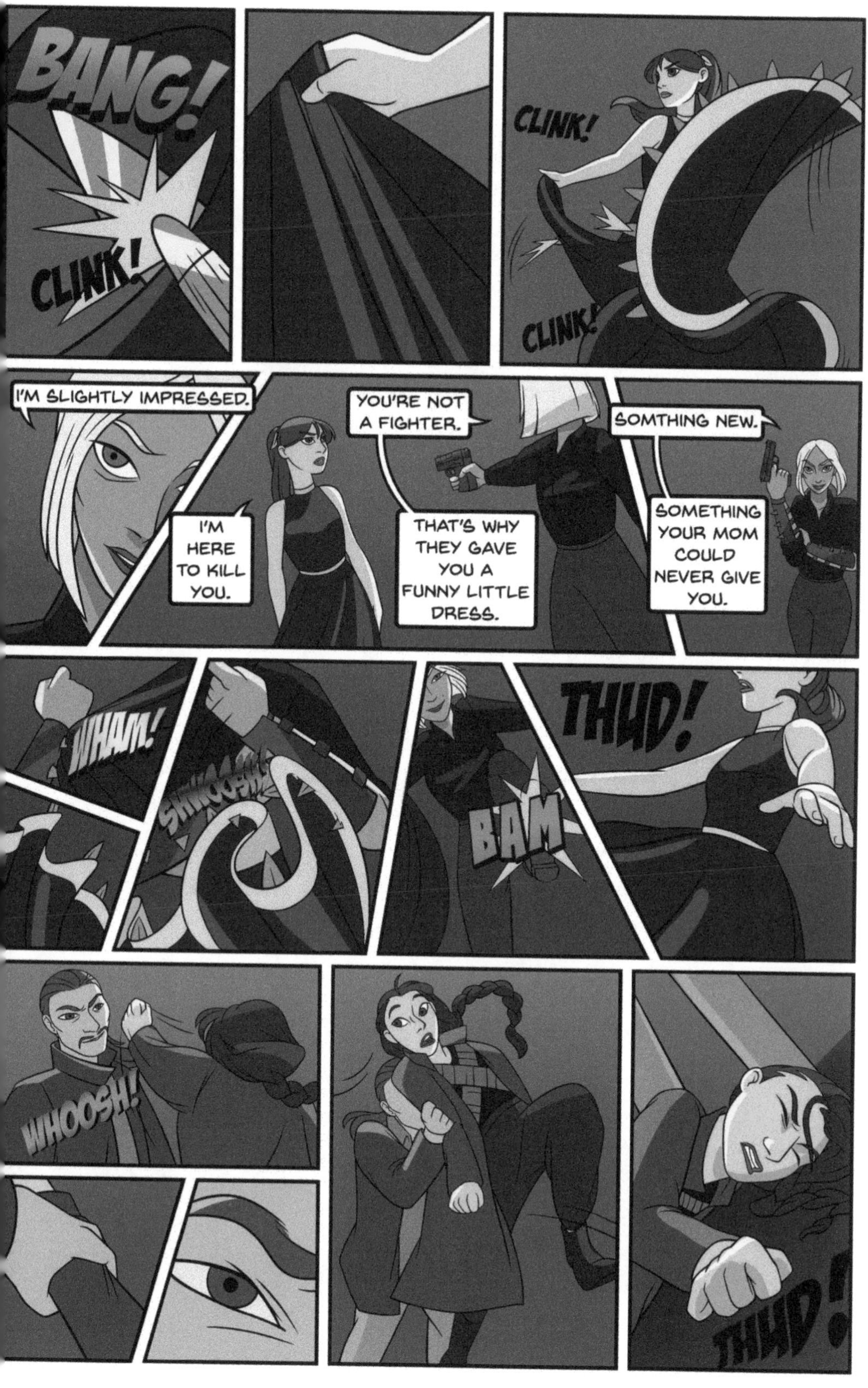
BANG!
CLINK!
CLINK!
CLINK!
I'M SLIGHTLY IMPRESSED.
I'M HERE TO KILL YOU.
YOU'RE NOT A FIGHTER.
THAT'S WHY THEY GAVE YOU A FUNNY LITTLE DRESS.
SOMTHING NEW.
SOMETHING YOUR MOM COULD NEVER GIVE YOU.
WHAM!
SHWOOSH!
BAM
THUD!
WHOOSH!
THUD!

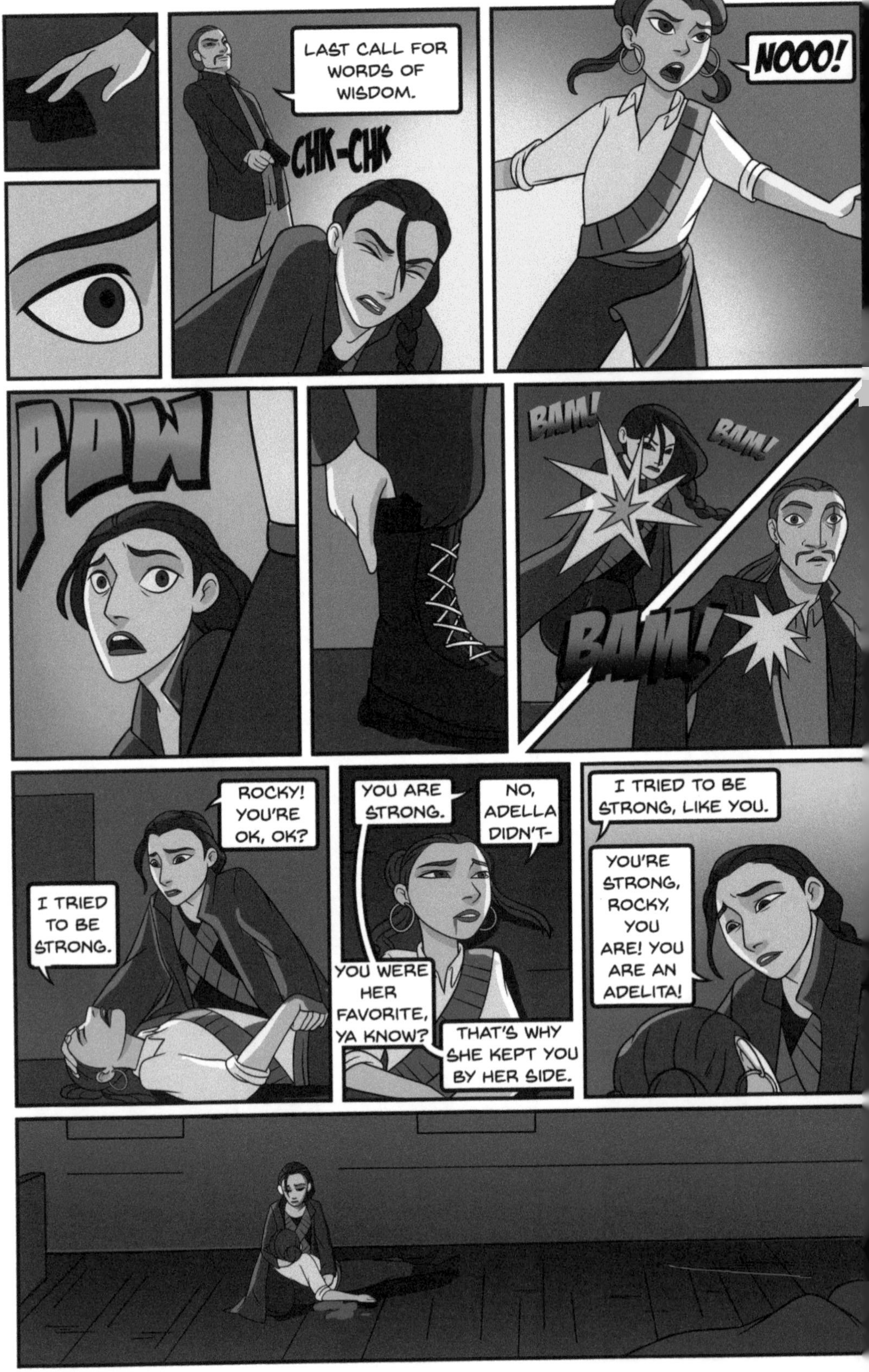

LAST CALL FOR WORDS OF WISDOM.
CHK-CHK
NOOO!
POW
BAM!
BAM!
BAM!
ROCKY! YOU'RE OK, OK?
I TRIED TO BE STRONG.
YOU ARE STRONG.
NO, ADELLA DIDN'T-
YOU WERE HER FAVORITE, YA KNOW?
THAT'S WHY SHE KEPT YOU BY HER SIDE.
I TRIED TO BE STRONG, LIKE YOU.
YOU'RE STRONG, ROCKY, YOU ARE! YOU ARE AN ADELITA!

CLANK!

SHWOORL

STOP!

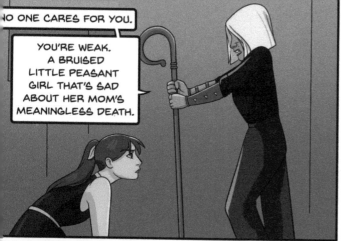

NO ONE CARES FOR YOU.

YOU'RE WEAK. A BRUISED LITTLE PEASANT GIRL THAT'S SAD ABOUT HER MOM'S MEANINGLESS DEATH.

AND THAT'S WHY I'M STRONGER THAN YOU.

DINK

DINK

KLGH!

KLGH!

CLANK!

WHERE'S ROCKY?

WE HAVE TO GET THE GIRLS OUT.

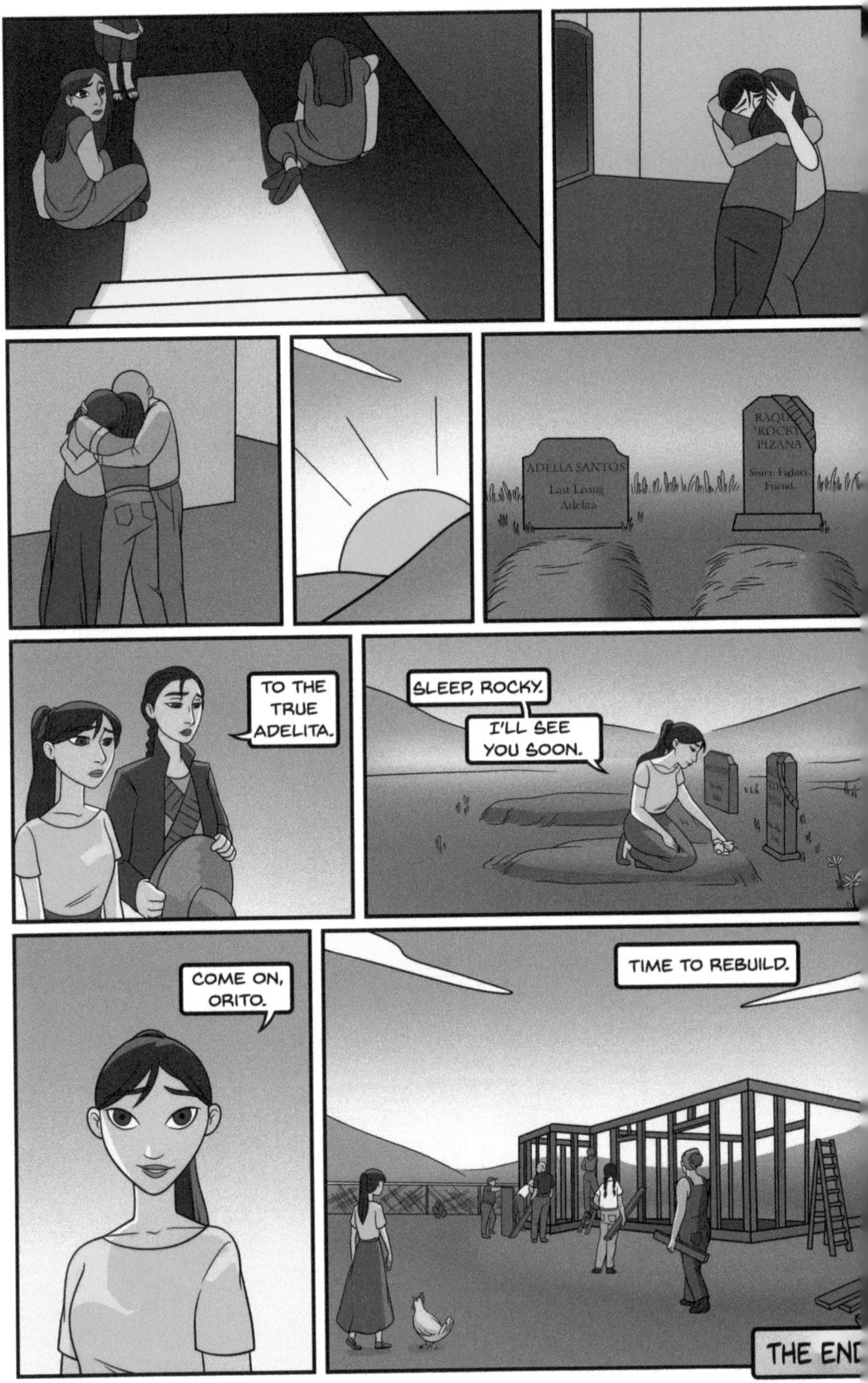
ADELLA SANTOS
Last Living
Adelita
PIZANA
Sister. Fighter.
Friend.
TO THE TRUE ADELITA.
SLEEP, ROCKY.
I'LL SEE YOU SOON.
COME ON, ORITO.
TIME TO REBUILD.

JALISCO

CONCEPT ART

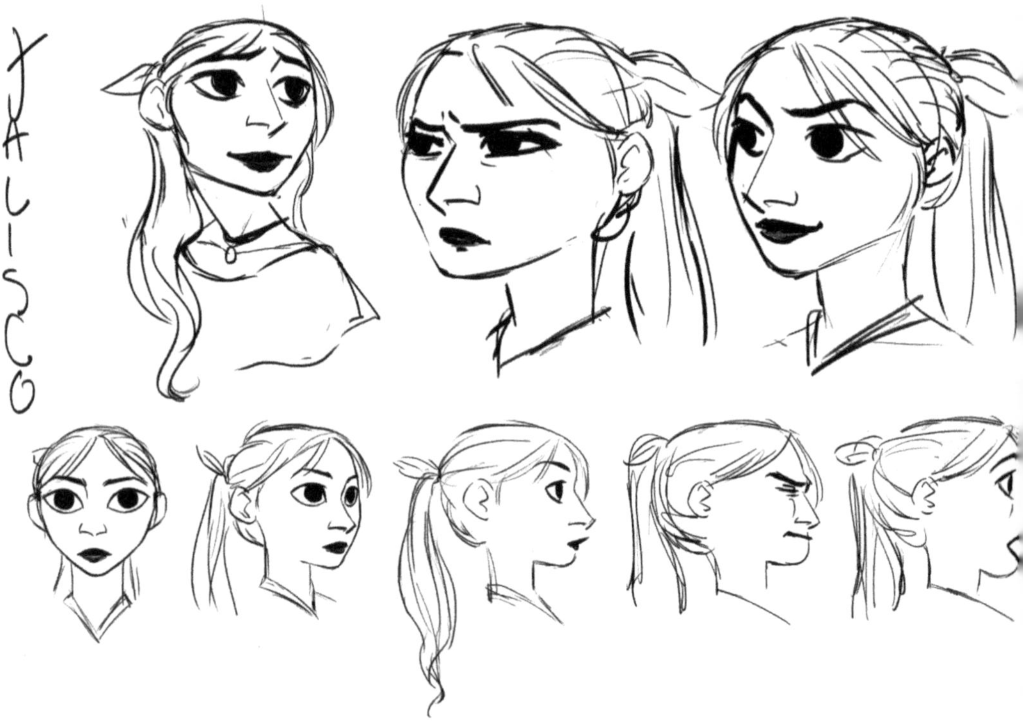
JALISCO

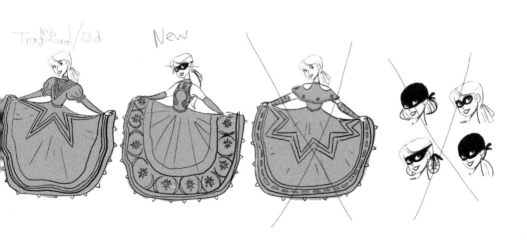

Traditional/old   New

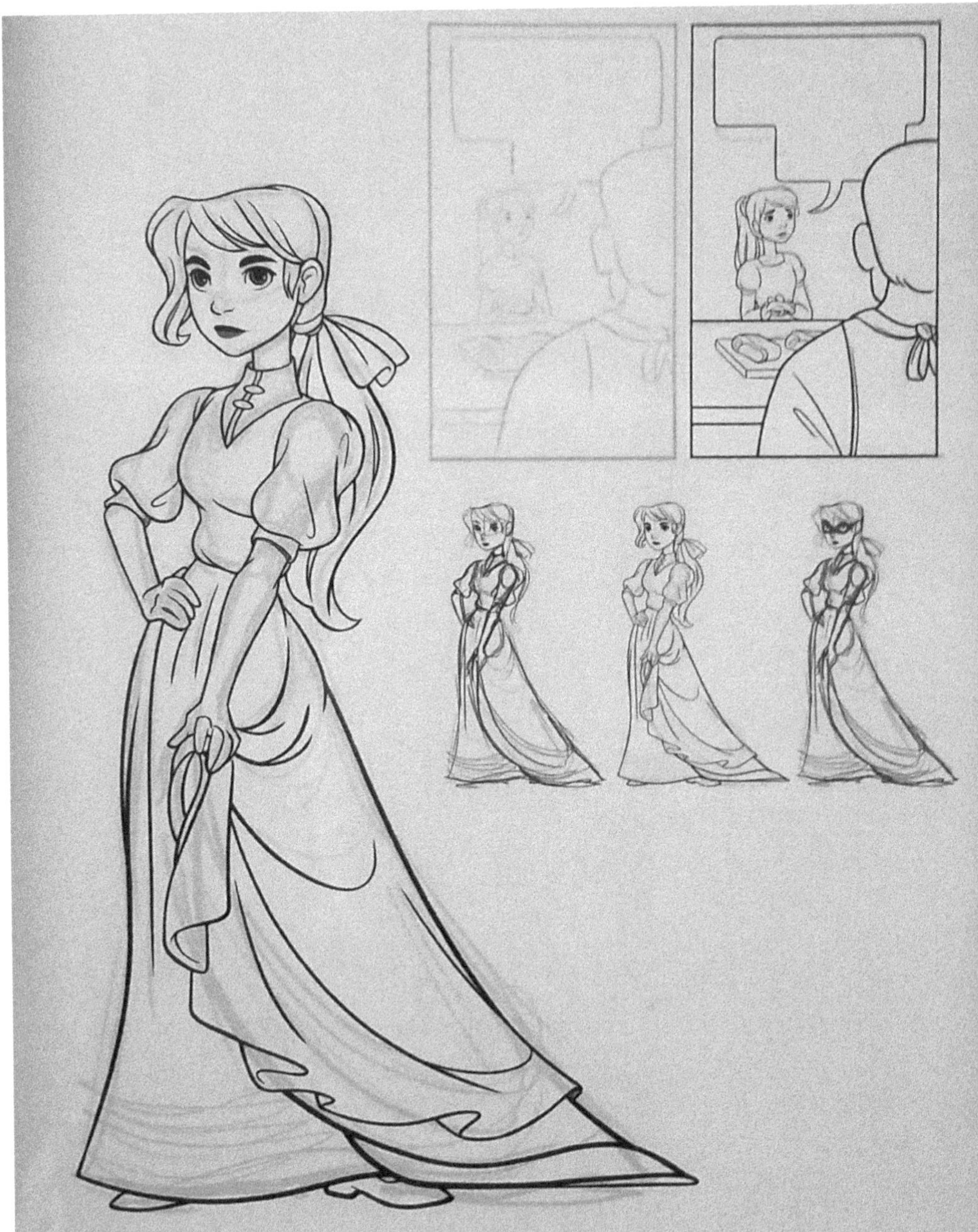

JALISCO   ROCKY   DELLA   MALINCHE   ADELA

More "Adelita" style

JALISCO   ROCKY   DELLA   MALINCHE   ADELA

90° MEXICAN FASHION

PANTS, COMBAT
BOOTS — COLLARED
TOPS, TANK TOPS

RIFLES

BANDOLIER
(FOR FINAL
FIGHT)

DICK!
— HAZEL
EYES

"MEXICAN CLOTH"
BELTS
SASHES

STUFF
HIDDEN
IN SASH!

FORM-FITTING

DELIA

TANK TOP + TRENCH COAT

20-30 ADELITTAS WHO GO OUT

NECK TATTOO
(FLOWERS?)

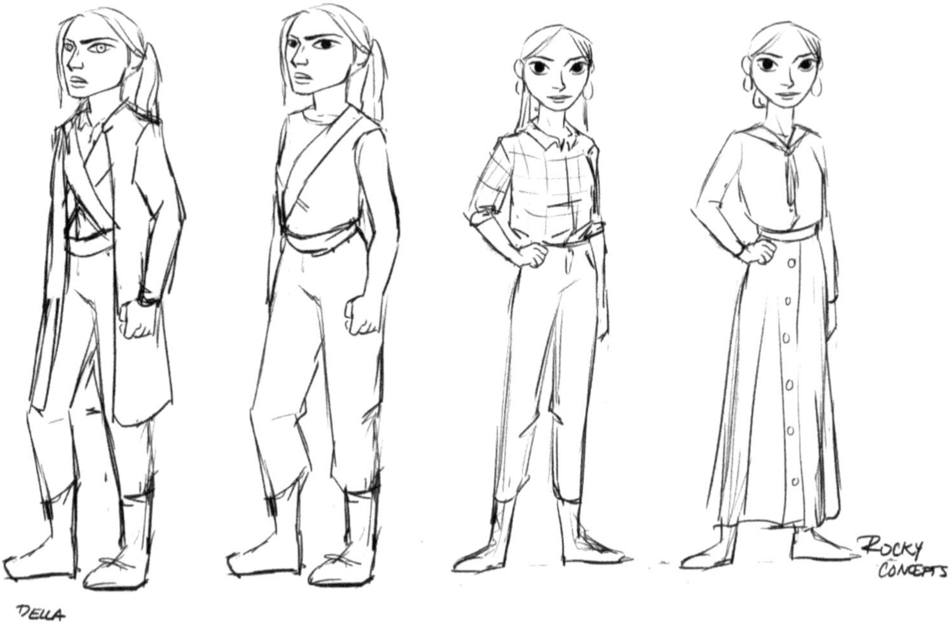
DELLA
ROCKY
CONCEPTS

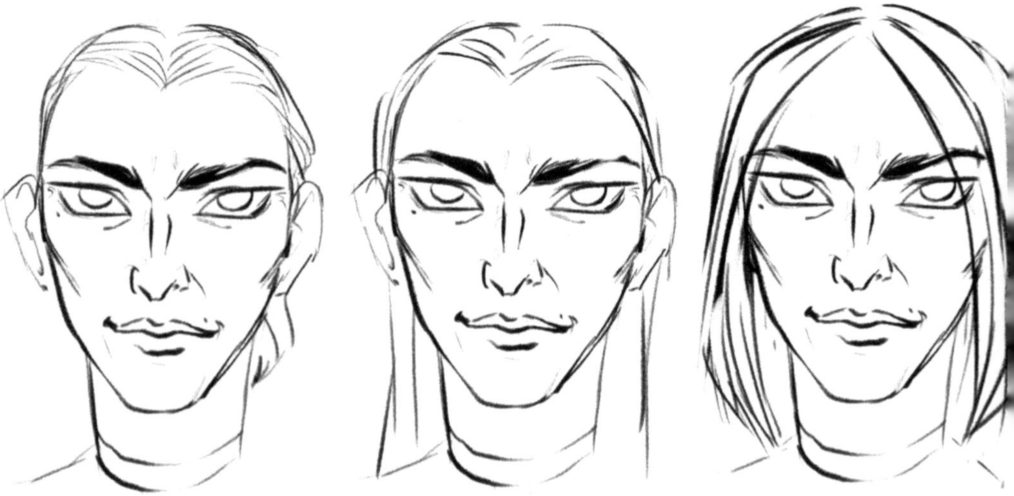

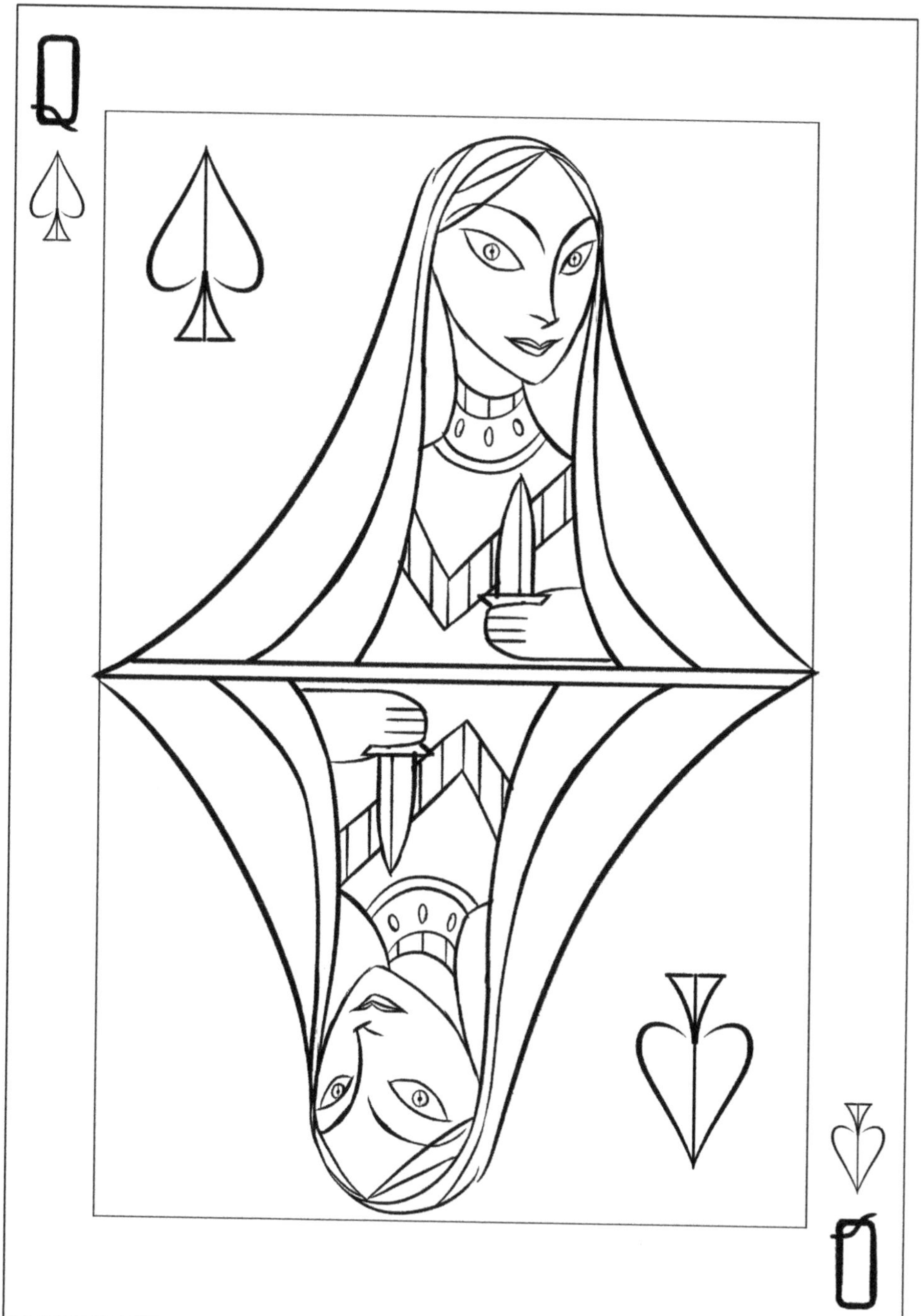

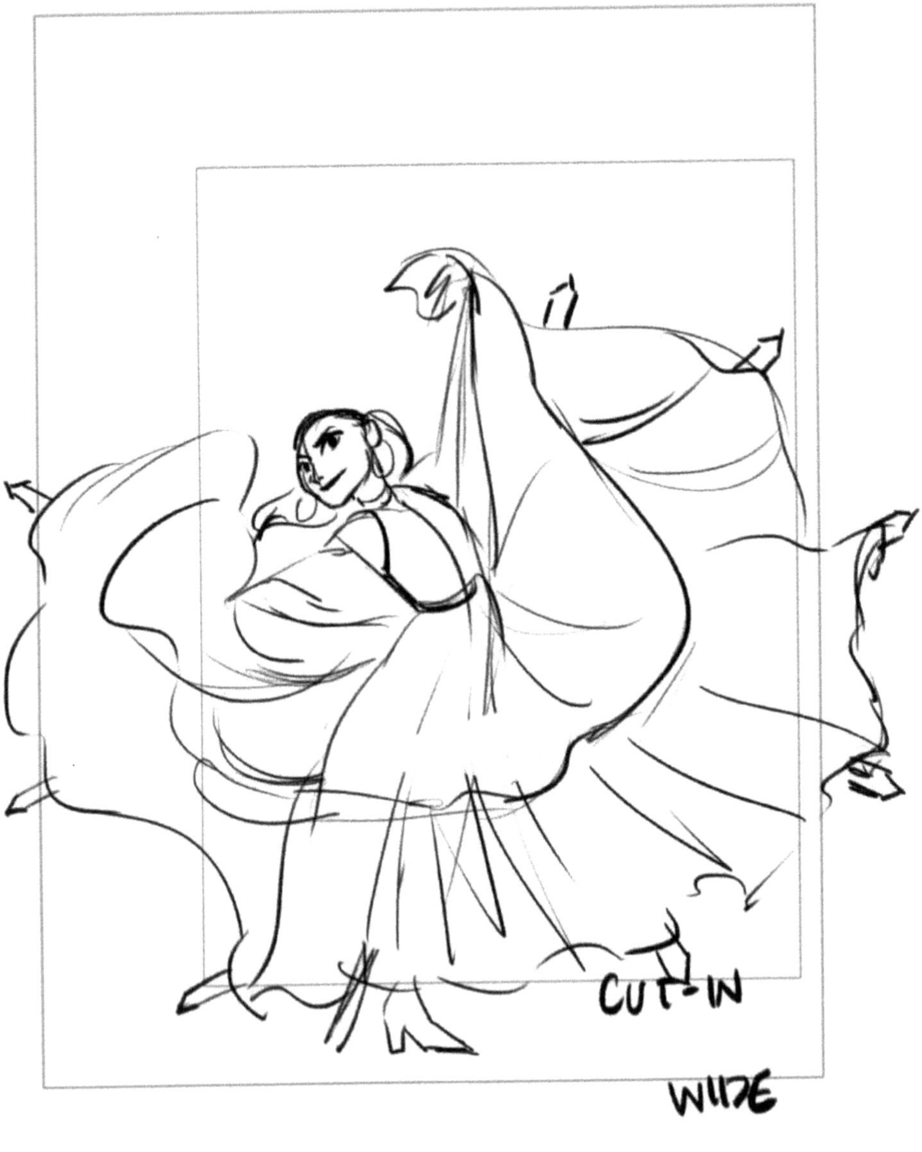
CUT-IN
WIDE

JALISCO

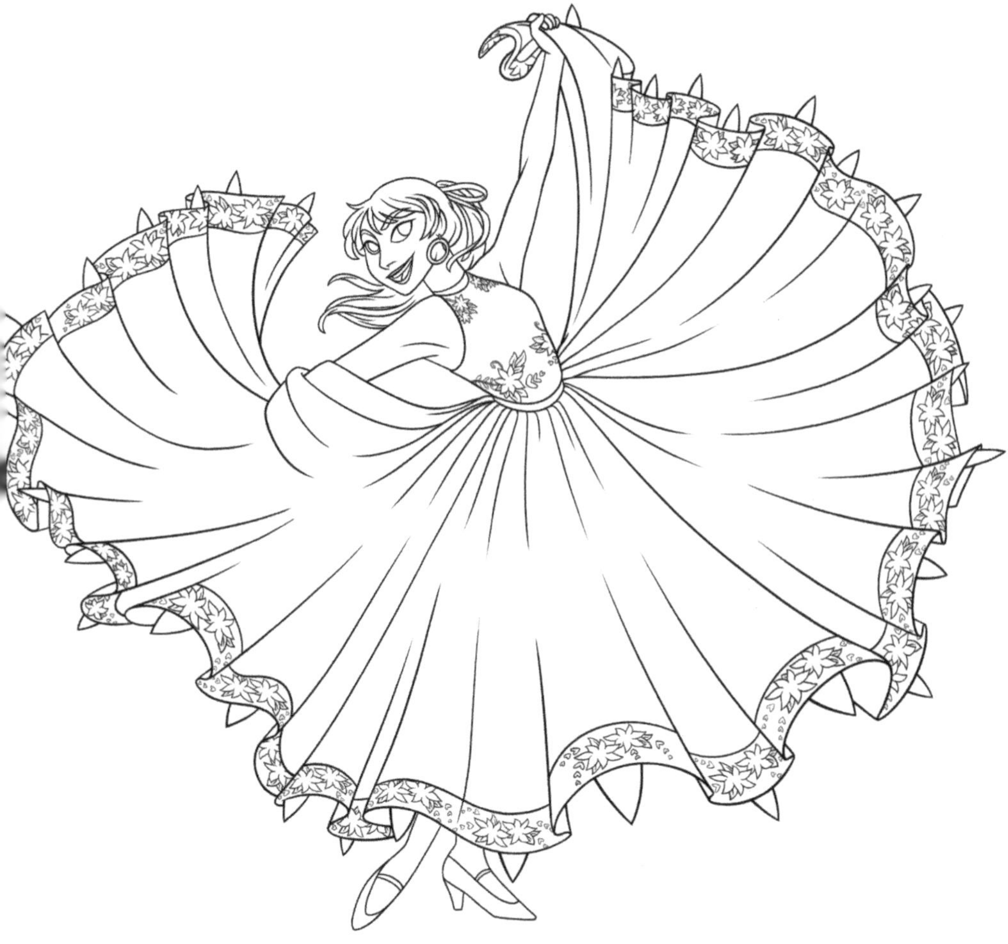